IN SEARCH OF SAIL
Tales of Short Sea Voyages

Robert Simper

Published in 1998 by Creekside Publishing
In association with

ISBN 0 9519927 8 3
Copyright R. Simper
Printed by Lavenham Press

By the same author

Over Snape Bridge (1967)
Woodbridge & Beyond (1972)
East Coast Sail (1972)
Scottish Sail (1974)
North East Sail (1975)
British Sail (1977)
Victorian & Edwardian Yachting from Old Photographs (1978)
Gaff Sail (1978)
Traditions of East Anglia (1979)
Suffolk Show (1981)
Britain's Maritime Heritage (1982)
Sail on the Orwell (1982)
Beach Boats of Britain (1984)
Sail: The Surviving Tradition (1984)
East Anglian Coast and Waterways (1985)
Suffolk Sandlings (1986)
The Deben River (1992)
The River Orwell and the River Stour (1993)
Rivers Alde, Ore and Blyth (1994)
Woodbridge: Pictorial History (1995)
Essex Rivers and Creeks (1995)
Norfolk Rivers and Harbours (1996)
Thames Tideway (1997)
River Medway and The Swale (1998)

CHAPTERS

Maps

INTRODUCTION

We had been going out herring drifting before Christmas. Really just an excuse for being on the boat. If we got a few in the bottom of a bucket to give everyone a 'feed' we were happy. I had intended to go again after Christmas, but the weather, as it often does, suddenly turned into real winter. *Three Sisters* remained tugging about on her mooring out in the river. All our family had departed for their homes, but someone had said 'you are always telling us about things you've done on boats, why don't you write them down ?'

Over the previous six years I had written seven books about the histories of the East Coast rivers. Hundreds of hours of detailed research so that it was very pleasant to just sit down and write without endless checking. Once I got going I found my memory full of blank spaces. Luckily I could draw on the log books, diaries and published accounts of these trips. I wondered how anyone who has not kept some kind of written record could ever write an accurate version of their life.

In my memory I recalled winning a race up the Thames in *L'Atalanta*, but it all seemed a little jumbled and I remember both running and tacking up the Thames. The log books clearly showed we had taken part in two separate races, a year apart. As *L'Atalanta's* long keel made running her best point of sailing we had won the second race. Even published material is not always reliable. I remember after the *Charlotte Rhodes* trip, a Belfast newspaper reporter came aboard and interviewed the skipper. In his account there were only five crew aboard, not six, even though I was standing beside him!

I owned *L'Atalanta* for twenty-three years and have spent more hours aboard her than any other boat, mostly uneventful family cruising which I have forgotten. The trips which stick in my mind are the ones where there were problems to be overcome. I have learned sailing and boat handling through making mistakes and then trying to avoid them.

This personal account of messing about in boats starts at the end of World War II, since then the world has changed completely. When it starts, working sail had just finished and I tried hard to catch a glimpse of this way of life before it was gone for ever. Much of my relentless sailing and searching since then has been in pursuit of traditional sailing vessels before they vanished. Increasingly in recent decades it has been to see the ships which have been restored. Although I have owned my own dinghies and boats since 1957 I have tried whenever possible every year to sail on at least one new boat type. Like this I have attempted to build up an understanding of working sailing craft. Sadly when I made a list of boats I have sailed on many are no longer in existence.

I am being deliberately out of date with this book and sticking to old measurements. It was the Anglo-Saxons who first found the length of a man's foot to be a useful measurement and the length of a man's stride to be a yard. This is fast becoming foreign to a new generation who have been taught the European metric system. To make this account more understandable it might be useful to know that feet is written as ft. and 3.28 feet equals one metre, while one mile is 1.609 kilometres.

This project has been greatly helped by editing and suggestions from Diana McMillan. As I have worked away at this book Pearl has often looked over my shoulder and made suggestions and corrections. Our son Jonathan has done the same. Why not, this is their story almost as much as it is mine.

L'Atalanta coming up the River Blackwater in the 1984 East Coast Old Gaffers' Race. (*Basil Emmerson*)

Paul's wooden barge *Marjorie* bound for Ipswich laden, skipper Mick Lungley, 1956.

Horlock's steel barge *Xylonite* with skipper Peter Light standing on the bowsprit in thigh boots, 1956.

Chapter One

LEARNING THE ROPES

The first time I remember going afloat the whole venture was cut short by soldiers firing at us. At the time the Suffolk coast, and all the East Coast of England, was dominated by World War II, although most of the action went on above our heads. In the night German bombers flew over us on their way to their targets and sometimes we saw our fighters trying to stop them. Towards the end of the war it just seemed to be American Super Fortresses going out on daytime bombing missions. I was hardly aware that we were near the sea because the whole coastal area was closed to the public. The high ground along the coast was dotted with anti-aircraft batteries, while all the beaches were mined to prevent invasion.

The family home at Bawdsey is at the end of a peninsula, with the sea on one side and the River Deben on the other. It was rather like growing up on an island, as there was only one road out across wild heathland to the little country town of the Woodbridge. Sometimes my mother would stand me on a farm gate and point to the waves rolling in through Hollesley Bay and say 'Look at the white horses today'.

The sea looked cold and decidedly mysterious, but I was intrigued by it.

As I grew older, we used to cycle down to Ramsholt Dock, an old barge quay on the Deben. I was delighted to play on the tiny beach. One day there were two teenage boys messing about in a dinghy and since I had shown enthusiasm for going out on the river my mother asked them if they would row us out to look at the battleship.

As we approached the huge grey vessel, soldiers suddenly appeared on deck and to our surprise started to fire over our heads. We headed straight back to shore and it was years before I learnt the truth about the 'battles ships'. In fact these were mock landing craft, several of which were moored in the Deben and Orwell rivers to kid the Germans that the D-Day landing was coming from this coast, although it was actually due to sail from the South Coast. The mock landing craft at Ramsholt was built on huge rafts in a wood behind Waldringfield and launched at night and towed down river. The men aboard actually lived ashore in huts in the middle of nearby Ramsholt School Wood.

The entrance to the Deben is a shallow channel over a bar through the shingle knolls. Without leading marks it can be hard to find in daylight, but in total war blackout it would have been very difficult to come over the bar safely. In the morning when the Felixstowe Ferry fishermen looked up the river and saw this huge naval craft off Ramsholt Dock they were convinced there was sometime very fishy about it. The talk in the 'Ferry Boat Inn' was that only a local man could have piloted a craft of that size in. Then the police arrived and told them firmly to keep their mouths shut and their thoughts to themselves!

After the war ended and the coast was opened up I made my first sea trips. These were in the Ford's open tripper boat from the Dip at Felixstowe out to the Cork lightship. Once it was rough and several small children in the boat were sick. Aft at the tiller one of the Ford family appeared totally removed from the human suffering and simply said 'it's wind over tide'.

I wondered what on earth this meant and was very keen to find out and learn the mysteries of the tides and coastal affairs. Shortly afterwards, a piece of luck took me afloat.

1. RS pushing the *Swallow*, a standing lug clinker dinghy he learned to sail in, down the mud beside Ramsholt Dock hard, 1953.

My father returned home with the news that an uncle of mine, John Garrard, had been given a fishing boat. His sisters had been GI brides and his whole family had emigrated to California, but although his father's butcher's shop in Alderton was sold, a buyer had not been found for his father's fishing boat. This was *Lassie*, an open Shingle Street beach boat, which was kept on a mooring at Ramsholt Dock and used to supply fresh fish for the shop. The *Lassie* had a bit of a problem with leaking so it became my job to row across the Deben and pump her out. Rowing across to *Lassie*, going out trawling and making family trips in her, started my passion for boats.

When in the late 1940s we used to go trawling at night in the *Lassie*, the river was a wide expanse of empty water and totally dark. Now the night sky is lit up with lights from Felixstowe, Ipswich and Woodbridge and on a very still night the roar of road traffic going down to the Port of Felixstowe can be heard. A more affluent age has filled just over half the distance of the tidal river with lines of yacht moorings. Although the Deben is now the most congested river on the East Coast, it is still an attractive river, but seems smaller because of the moorings. Only in the middle of winter, when virtually all the boats are ashore, can you see the natural river. Even then the river is dotted with a mass of brightly-coloured mooring buoys.

The *Lassie's* maintenance was entrusted to Arthur Hunt, a man who had run away to sea about in 1904 on a ketch barge discharging coal at Ramsholt. Arthur wore a smock, peaked cap and had a face which was brown and wrinkled by the weather so that it looked like a walnut. In spite of this very healthy appearance, he was not a well man and did not live to be a great age. During World War I he had been bosun on a ship torpedoed in the Adriatic. In order to save the ship Arthur took a party of 'Lasers', Indian seamen, down into the hold to move the cargo, which unfortunately when it became wet was to give off fumes. These fumes killed several of the men, but Arthur survived, losing one lung. His

2. Arthur Hunt splicing a new sheet on *Sea Fever*. These were sisal and had to be renewed every year, 1957. A bottle of rum is being held up to get Arthur to smile.

health eventually forced him to give up deep sea ships and he returned to Suffolk to become a Deben boatman, heavy work which he found difficult. When I was about fifteen Arthur was very pleased to take me with him to do the rowing and help when lifting yacht moorings.

The best times with Arthur were in the winter, when he made nets by hand for the Aldeburgh fishermen. His main job was as skipper of the Gilby's yacht, the *Genesta,* and in the winter when she was laid up against Ramsholt Dock quay he used her cabin as a workshop. There was only one house and a pub at Ramsholt Dock and the place was very deserted during the winter. Arthur was there every day, working away in the lonely yacht cabin and was very glad to have someone to talk to. The tilly lamp hissed away throwing a soft light on Arthur's face while his hands worked quickly and the net grew before us. I started asking questions: 'what was it like when you went to sea Arthur ?'

Arthur loved it. Like many sailors he was a born storyteller and an Edwardian seascape of eastern England opened up before me, with tales of long-gone barges and how he joined the West country schooner *Alert,* which had been in the Newfoundland dry cod trade. Years later someone in San Francisco wrote an enthusiastic review about one of my books - he thought it had captured the age of sail perfectly and assumed I must have been in these ships. I was not old enough by fifty years, but had gained a very real understanding of that age carefully listening to story after story about barges, schooners and then how Arthur had 'left the sea and gone into steam'.

Arthur retained all the prejudices and superstitions of a man trained in sail, whose whole life was dictated by the winds which seemed to be controlled by dark forces which should not be offended. In World War II Arthur used to go fishing in the *Lassie* with Jack Garrard. Once they were trawling off the Deben a few days after a Dutch ferry making for Harwich was sunk with heavy loss of life. A woman's body came up in the trawl and they thought 'we don't want anything to do with this' and put her back. Next morning, when Arthur went down to Ramsholt Dock, there was the woman's body lying on the mud near his boat. She had followed them up the river.

Once as we passed Walton Pier a distress rocket was fired from a small yacht, only because her elderly crew were unable to get the anchor up. This was not a major rescue, but we hung around until the RNLI Lifeboat came around the pier.

'Look at the longshore sharks !' cried Arthur in real anger 'Quick to prey on the poor sailor.'

To us, this seemed a strange prejudice against men who had given up their time freely to help others. Arthur, however, had been at sea when East Anglian beach companies had extracted every penny they could get out of ships in distress. Before 1914 Felixstowe Ferry had a small salvage company run by the Newsons, who kept a galley in front of the Martello Tower. Because there was no RNLI lifeboat at Felixstowe Ferry, and yachts were for ever getting ashore on the Deben Bar, the tradition of salvaging lived on here longer than anywhere else on the East Coast. A hut near the Sailing Club often had its door open and a watch was kept by telescope. Once a yacht hit the bar or the shingle knolls a launch would race down to give help for a negotiated fee.

My first trip as a crew on the open sea was with the Rev. Will Groom on his 43ft schooner *Lora*, a splendid yacht built by Dickie on the west coast of Scotland in 1907. Standing at the tiller of the *Lora* Will Groom looked like a pirate, because he had lost an eye in a motorbike accident and wore a patch over the empty socket. His duties with the Church of England kept him busy on Saturdays and Sundays, so he had all week to go trawling. However, since most people worked during the week he had difficulties in finding a crew and was very glad to take a keen young teenager along.

Providing you liked boats and fishing, the Rev. Will was a great character, although some of his Hollesley parishioners thought they should see more of him. It was rumoured that funerals and mother's union meetings were scheduled so that they did not interfere with good tides for getting the *Lora* over the Deben Bar.

Trips with the *Lora* started in the tiny bar of the Ramsholt 'Arms', then run by an old lady called Mrs Nunn. She, poor old thing, had bad feet, so she used to ask us regulars to go down into the cellar and draw our own beer. Since I was well below the legal limit of going into pubs, this was a real adventure.

'Don't you have too much, boy Robert' the old lady used to shout from her stool behind the bar 'I can see you'. But actually she couldn't see how much Cobbolds bitter I drew.

By the time we rowed across river, the *Lora's* crew would be in a very merry frame of mind. Once a suitcase was dropped in the water and everyone was laughing so much that they had difficulty fishing it out. Early next morning we headed off down river over the Deben bar and out to the Hollesley Bay fishing grounds.

It was on the *Lora* that I was first seasick. As usual, we met the pilot Newson at the Deben entrance and followed his boat *Della* through the tricky channel over the Bar. The Rev. Will muttered something about it always being best to pay the pilot so that you knew he would be there when you needed him. On the day of the seasickness we had motored out into an angry grey sea, but we still turned towards Hollesley Bay. I was put on the tiller, one minute the *Lora's* bow pointed towards the sky and the next it crashed into a sea. To try and make it more comfortable Rev Will hoisted the gaff foresail, but like most of the schooner's gear, it had seen better days and split. It was far to lumpy to trawl, but being a deep-draught yacht we could not get back into the Deben until the next high tide, some twelve hours later.

4

In the end the relentless motion got the better of me. After being sick in the tiny heads in the bows I lay on a bunk watching a loaf of bread sliding around the cabin floor, vowing I would never go to sea again. But I could not get away from boats. I used to go to the school library and read all I could about them. All the books were quite definite that sailing ships had all finished, which I believed until the day my grandfather Turner decided to take me around Ipswich Dock. I think he was trying to show me the big mills and maltings which were the centre of the local farming economy. But it was sailing barges lying on the berths in front of the mills that caught my eye. This was in the early 1950s and the two Ipswich milling firms, Pauls and Cransfields, still kept their fleets of barges to bring grain up from the London docks.

After this, when we went to Ipswich on Market Days, I used to go down to the docks on my own. Often there were half a dozen sailing barges lying between freights in front of the Custom House. The smoke from the fo'c'sle chimneys drifted up through the rigging and past the lofty varnished topmasts. One day I got into conversation with Gordon Hardy, skipper of the sailing barge *George Smeed*, and another time I helped him when he was on a charter moving grain from a ship on Cliff Quay up to the mills. He promised, next time he came to Ipswich, to take me away to the London River. I waited, but never heard from him, and when I phoned the owner's office in Colchester they sounded rather surprised and said they had recently scrapped all their sailing barges. I realised that if I was going to taste the age of sail I should be quick, because the barges were all going to be finished soon.

The Ipswich grain barges were crewed by two hands, usually an elderly skipper and a school-leaver as mate, but nearly always from the town. After a lot of phoning I heard that the *Will Everard*, a steel auxiliary mulie barge which could load 295 tons and was normally manned by a skipper and three hands, was at King's Lynn, but there were only three aboard. Early one still morning in September 1955 I threw my kit bag and thigh boots down on the steel decks of the *Will Everard* as she lay in the Custom's House Creek. She was loaded with 240 tons of Norfolk wheat and was waiting for the tide to float her so that she could leave for Hull. Once down the ladder on the deck I lowered my sea bag and thigh boots in to the fo'c'sle. There were two young men in the bunks and neither spoke for some time. Then the mate Cyril Wright said in his best Suffolk:

'What are the boots for - expect sea aboard ?'

At seventeen, I was totally humiliated by the remark about my thigh boots. On fishing trips these had been very practical, but coasting bargemen, it seems, went to sea in clothes more suited to an outing to the cinema than to the open North Sea. I was labelled a fisherman and hid my thigh boots, but there were times when I could have worn them. One night when the barge was deeply loaded bound for the Humber, it came on to blow really hard. We fought in the dark to get the topsail down with the water rolling aboard almost up to the mastcase. Another night, bound laden for the Humber, there was so much water on the deck that we could not go forward to call the cook, Nobby, for his watch with the skipper. Instead, we watched the white water crashing along the deck in the moonlight washing almost up to the wheelhouse where we remained. I could have worn my sea boots then, but I didn't.

Everards had this barge on long charter delivering wheat from Lynn to the Co-op Mills in the Old Harbour, Hull. Going up the Old Harbour just before high water was rather a picnic, because there were constant near misses with keels and coasters coming down. Although we topped the bowsprit up, it once got caught in a warehouse chute and with the

3. The *Will Everard* on passage with coal from Keadby to Harwich Gas Works about 1958.

tide pushing the barge up it looked as if we were going to damage the warehouse. Cyril, like myself an escapee from a Suffolk farm, jumped up on the rail and worked like mad to cut us clear. Another time, going up on a dark night, we almost ran a keel down. They should have carried navigation lights, but this one just had a keelman standing in the bow with a bicycle torch. As we moved past in the night a Yorkshire voice explained bluffly that the torch battery had gone flat.

4. The steel barge *Will Everard* at the Co-op Mills, Old Harbour, Hull, 1955.

Skipper Paddy O'Donald liked to keep the food bill down under a pound a head so the mate Cyril, an old sea dog at eighteen, and the sixteen year old cook Nobby from Gillingham, used to shoot off and buy pies from a shop near the Co-op Mills. I was never sure about those pies, and did not take part in the feast. Once going back to Lynn at night Cyril complained of bad stomach ache and went out on the deck to be sick. As he went out of the wheelhouse he gave me the compass course and said, 'remember it is the barge that moves, not the compass', then he was gone and I was alone.

I was still trying to work out what he meant when I got hold of the huge wheel. For a while all went well, my relationship with the bows of the barge and compass seemed to be successful, but like all beginners I used the wheel too much and suddenly the head seemed to be going in the wrong direction and then the barge gybed. I fought madly and got the head going in the other direction and over went the gear in another mighty crash as it gybed the other way.

The skipper lived down in the aft cabin below the wheelhouse and suddenly there was a burst of angry shouting, ' Cyril, Cyril what the devil do you think you are doing' came the rich Ulster voice of our barge master. In no time he was by my side cursing the poor Cyril for gorging on pies. Shortly afterwards we picked up the pilot near Lynn Well and he, poor man, was less able to steer a barge downwind than I had been. Paddy could do no more that mutter in the background about what the owners would do if there was any damage to the gear.

I had hoped to make some form of photographic record of a ship working under sail while I was aboard the *Will Everard*. In fact, I only had a cheap camera and to make matters worse I took it into my head to effect some repairs because it did not appear to be functioning correctly. I started taking it to pieces on the fo'c'sle table, but the vibration of the engine caused the little screws to bounce on to the floor. This really ended my first attempt at photography for posterity.

Although the barge went on carrying cargoes for another ten years, the economic world it belonged to was slowly passing.

Even in the mid-1950s the *Will Everard* was a good money-earner for her owners and crew, but to achieve this, on passage the diesel engine was kept running all the time, although she was handled as a sailing vessel. We tacked to windward with the engine running. Back at home, I told Arthur Hunt about this and he shook his head sadly and said that was no good and if I was going to learn how to work sail properly I would have to go in a barge without an engine. I set off to Ipswich and found that Gordon Hardy, after the *George Smeed* was 'cut down' to a lighter, had become skipper of the steel sailing barge *Portlight*. Gordon told me he needed a mate and to return in a few days when he had orders where to go next. I did, but found he had taken on Harold Mann as mate, but he had arranged that I should go over to Mistley where Peter Light needed a mate on *Xylonite*, a barge which loaded about 125 tons.

'Been in a barge before?' asked Peter. I said I had been to the Humber on the *Will Everard*. He laughed and said 'Well the furthest I've been in a barge is Yarmouth!' His voice raised when he mentioned Great Yarmouth because this bar haven's entrance could be a difficult one in bad weather so it was much respected by bargemen, but I don't think he was all that impressed. At twenty-two he was quite capable of sailing the barge by himself. Indeed sometimes he seemed to forget I was there and just carried on. He was a quiet man and what was more, he wore thigh boots for boat work. Unlike the *Will Everard*, where earning money was the name of the game, Peter cared little about cash and just-

5. The only other auxiliary barge in the Wash-Humber trade was London & Rochester's *Thyra*. Here she is leaving Wisbech down the River Nene laden with wheat for the Co-Op Mills, Hull. She had a crew of two while the large *Will Everard* had four, 1955.

9

wanted to go on sailing a barge as long as possible. So too did Gordon and about half a dozen other young men on the last working sailing barges.

It was also a mistake to have said I had been on a barge, because although at that time I knew how the gear worked, I could not find the toilet on *Xylonite*. On the *Will Everard* there had been a rather primitive toilet in the wheelhouse, but it was not until I saw the skipper going down the fo'c'sle with a bucket with some water in it that I realised this was the toilet. Everything about the barge was pure Victorian technology, very simple and very effective.

Sailing barges only made their passage when the conditions were favourable, namely a 'fair' wind or tide, this meant they spent a lot of time 'wind bound' at anchor. Once, when anchored in a fog, we realised Peter's portable radio battery was flat and that evening it was the 'Goon Show'. To have missed this cultural highlight of the week was unthinkable. Peter, a born sailor, did a fine point of navigation by finding our way through the fog in the barge's boat to where the *Portlight* was at anchor with a working radio.

As mate, it was my duty to do the cooking. I was OK on frying and heating up tins of beans, but any further than that and I was in trouble. Since sailing barges spent a lot of time anchored in remote places waiting for a fair wind, several skippers developed a passion for shooting. Once the *Marjorie* was seen stalking duck under sail, the mate at the wheel and the skipper with a shotgun forward crouched under the bit heads hoping to creep up on duck sitting on the water. Another time, the mates brushed up Shotley marshes in the fog for the skippers to shoot hares, but they did not shoot anything. Then one morning Gordon and Peter returned in the boat from a wildfowling trip very triumphant that they had shot a mallard.

6. Peter Light on the Mistley spritsail barge *Xylonite*. He was watching Harold Mann on *Portlight* sounding with the lead line as we found our way up the Thames in a fog, 1956.

I was given the task of cooking it. Sitting on the forehatch I plucked the duck with feathers blowing away in the wind, but I got the fo'c'sle stove roaring away and over-cooked the bird. When I showed Peter the charred duck remains he threw it overboard and said solemnly 'we had better put it back in its rightful place.'

'When we are gone' said Gordon sadly talking about the remaining sailing barges, 'all the boat work will finish. Look at the motor barges, they never take their boats off the hatches, let alone sail them like we do.'

Gordon was a Londoner who had built a canoe and with his brother had set off down the Thames. In the Lower Hope the canoe had been swamped and a passing barge, skippered by Hedley Farrington, had rescued them and hauled the canoe up on to the hatches. By the time they arrived at Colchester, Gordon had fallen under the spell of barges and decided he was going to try and keep them sailing as long as possible.

Everyone knew that working cargoes under sail in Europe was going to finish and one by one the sailing barges dropped out, so there would never be any chance of repeating the experience of working sail. Most of the men barging for a career had long since moved over to motor barges, where the money was much better. There was a tremendous feeling of comradeship during those final years of the Thames barges in working sail.

In November 1956 a spell of stiff north-easterly winds prevented all the remaining sailing barges which came down from the London docks from sailing. They anchored 'wind bound' at Sheerness. They were all bound for the mills at Ipswich or Mistley and were waiting for a 'slant' of fair wind to get down the coast. In order to make the passage up the coast the barges had to pass through the Spitway, a narrow channel between two sand-

7. The steel barge *Xylonite* loading bags of sunflower seed out of the cargo ship *St John's* at Bellamy's, Rotherhithe, 1956.

banks, which was very shallow at low tide. The skippers had to plan their passages to arrive at the Spitway when there was enough water for them to go through. No one left, particularly not in the winter, until they were certain they would get through the Spitway safely.

The crew of the barges passed the days 'ship visiting' by boat and the great talking point was the sinking of the *Colonia,* which a few weeks earlier had sunk near the Pollard Spit off the Swale. She was the last Kent owned barge trading under sail.

As the days wore on the skipper of the *Spinaway C* came over and stated that, like us, they were running out of coal for the cabin fire. Bargemen lived off the land as much as possible and favoured acquiring coal from Cory's lighters rather than purchasing it. In this case all eyes turned to the Admiralty coal hulk *Agincourt*, a ram-bowed iron-clad dating from 1865, which was moored over on the Sheerness shore. After dark we set out in our two barge's boats and climbed up the high sides of the *Agincourt*. The two watchmen down in the massive stern cabin looked slightly alarmed when we marched in and explained our mission. They were given a tip not to come on deck and we set about the task of filling our sacks with coal and lowering them into the boat. The cabin fire burned very brightly that night.

Once when Peter was ashore and I was down in the stern cabin reading, the laden barge suddenly heeled as if she was under full sail. Going on deck I found a hurricane force wind was blowing and the *Spinaway C* and another barge were dragging across the river. Shortly afterwards, *Xylonite* started to move. Peter had rigged a second anchor and had it ready for such an occasion. I let it go and the barge stopped.

Later, when the wind dropped, Peter returned and we tried to recover the second anchor, but it had fouled on something on the bottom and we could not get it up. That night all the bargemen came aboard and, directed by Jim Lawrence, skipper of the *Memory*, who went out on the bowsprit, their combined strength on the winch handles brought up our second anchor plus an ancient Admiralty patent one that it had fouled. The next day the Admiralty anchor was ferried ashore and we tried to persuade the Receiver of Wrecks to pay us for it. As they would have nothing to do with this anchor we left it sitting on Sheerness Hard.

I was woken just before dawn next morning by Peter who said the wind had dropped and we were going for Harwich. Around us in the dark was the noise of eight windlasses as all the barges got under way and the dark shapes of their sails silhouetted against the dawn sky. Over a thousand tons of cargo was on the move, but there was not a sound. Well, apart from the skipper of *Spinaway C* cursing his mate for being slow to get up and they were going to be last away. Heading for the open estuary were the *Anglia, Marjorie, May, Memory, Portlight, Spinaway C, Venture* and of course *Xylonite.* These were the remaining barges genuinely working under sail, apart from the *Cambria* which was lying in the Thames waiting for a freight. There were of course many sailing barges still trading that were fitted with engines, but these were, in the eyes of the sailorman, classified as motor barges.

Not long afterwards Horlocks laid up the *Xylonite* and *Portlight*, so that was the last time so many barges in trade sailed in company, but this was a story that had been going on for decades. After every gale, every Board of Trade survey, another sailing barge dropped out until eventually there were only motor barges left and even they slowly declined with the competition from road transport.

In 1964 Gordon Hardy gave me a ring and asked if I would crew on the *Memory* in the Pin Mill Barge Match, one of the races for barges sailed for pleasure. This was a totally

8. Gordon Hardy at the wheel of the sailing barge *Portlight* which was laden with fish meal and bound from London to Ipswich. Gordon's Lambretta motor bike is in the stern, 1956. (*Graham Hussey*)

different world. In the trading days there were usually only the skipper and mate going off to their craft in the barge's boats. At the bottom of Pin Mill hard barge's boats were loaded with cheerful people in bright new oilskins being ferried out to the waiting barges. On the *Memory* there was mass of people, both passengers and crew, and the start of the race was a leisurely affair. The skipper for the day, Hedley Farrington, had skippered barges in trade and really did not see the importance of being first over the starting line.

In that Pin Mill race we spent the day sailing at the tail end of the fleet with *Salcote Belle*. Hedley Farrington said we should all enjoy the sight of the barges sailing because in a few years time these craft would all be worn out and gone. Now the poor old *Memory* and *Salcote Belle* are just rotting hulks abandoned in the saltings at Tollesbury, but the races kindled the enthusiasm of many people to move heaven and earth to try to keep them sailing. The flat-bottomed spritsail is an amazingly versatile craft. For two hundred years they had been a cheap form of bulk transport, but when this was over they were easily adapted to yachts, holiday charter and promotion barges. Decades after their original purpose finished the sight of brown sails above the river walls is still a common sight on the east of England. It is unthinkable that sailing barges should ever be allowed to die out.

Kings Lynn

NORFOLK

Great Yarmo

Gorleston

Lowestoft

Blythburgh

Southwold

Dunwich

Snape

Thorpeness

SUFFOLK

Aldeburgh

Orford

Orfordness

Woodbridge

Ipswich

Shingle Street

Pin Mill

Ramsholt

Mistley

Felixstowe Ferry

Harwich

Colchester

The Naze

ESSEX

Tollesbury

Brightlingsea

Maldon

West Mersea

Osea Island

SPITWAY

Stone Point

Lower Hope

RIVER THAMES

Gillingham

Sheerness

Lower Halstow

KENT

Chapter Two

OVER THE OTHER SIDE

By 1956 there were about fifteen yachts kept at Ramsholt and most Sunday nights the keener boating types would meet for a chat in the tiny bar of the 'Arms'. There was the hiss of the oil Tilly lamp which gave a gentle light over part of the room. Mrs Nunn sat on her stool behind the bar while there was an unwritten rule that the corner seat near the window was occupied by George Cook, the parish's oldest inhabitant.

At one of these gatherings on a raw March night, Eric Burley leant across to me and said 'Would you like to come and help get the *Tenace* back from Antwerp. Your experience with leeboards could be helpful'. My knowledge of leeboards was limited to the fact that they were very hard work to heave up on a winch, but I accepted the offer at once to join the trip, as you could not call yourself a sailor on the east coast then until you had been 'over the other side' of the North Sea.

The *Tenace* was a hoogaars, a flat-bowed barge used for fishing in the shallow Ooster and Wester Schelde. *Tenace* had been built in the 1930s as a yacht and had been sailed by her Belgian owner with a paid hand. Actually the Dutch fishermen had abandoned their traditional craft and it was the yachtsmen of Antwerp who had kept these craft going. However, Eric Burley, who loved a new boat with a challenge, bought her and eight of us went over to bring her back to Ramsholt.

The previous owner was an Antwerp diamond merchant and he had agreed to come and sail with us down the Wester Schelde River. Before the war *Tenace* had been sailed without an engine by his father, so as soon as we got out of the yacht haven the engine was cut and we began to tack down river in amongst the shipping. Aft, the diamond merchant leant on the huge tiller puffing away at his cigar, but kept a watchful eye on the stream of huge inland waterways barges that thundered past.

'Before the war' said our expert skipper 'these barges were handled by men who started in sail. Now look at them' he cried in despair as another great barge passed far too close to us 'they don't understand sail at all !'

The plan had been to reach Zeebrugge on the first day, but the ebb tide had finished and we were still in the Schelde, so we went into Terneuzen. This was then a peaceful little fishing village and we all went up into a cafe to enjoy a meal.

'Wait' said our diamond merchant skipper, 'in the late evening they still come out and promenade here, like in the old days'. He was right, in the days before television, the people of Terneuzen came out on to the main street in the evening and 'promenaded', walked up and down talking to their friends and neighbours. It was a lovely place, although I doubt whether with all the gossiping that must have gone on anyone ever kept a secret there. The only other place I have witnessed this is in Venice. There the people came out into the squares in the evening and talked and laughed with their friends.

In Terneuzen I bought a pair of clogs. The clog maker handed me a pair, but when they would not fit he took them back and cut some wood out so that they did. I tried to wear the Dutch clogs (and later Danish ones), but could never get on with them. At that time clogs were the standard footwear for country people in the Netherlands. We sailed via Zeebrugge back across the North Sea to Harwich, where we went into the Pound to clear Customs.

9. Aboard the hoogaars *Tenace* beating down the Wester Schelde River. Former Belgian owner at the tiller and Eric Burley on the right, 1956.

At school we had learned about America, Canada and Australia, but no one ever mentioned the Low Countries. Yet these European countries were only a few hours sailing from where I lived and I knew nothing about them. The Netherlands and its waterways seemed immensely attractive and I was determined to sail there and see more.

The next winter I began looking for a yacht to buy. Sitting in the East Coast Yacht Agency in Woodbridge I was shown details of all the yachts on sale on the local rivers. My heart sunk, even a little 4 tonner I looked at in the Walton Backwaters was £450 and I could never find that sort of money. They came up with one I could afford at Maylandsea. We went see the *White Heather,* a wonderful Edwardian gaff cutter of around 32ft long. We climbed aboard and found the cabin knee-deep in water and smelling of rotten wood. I began to wonder if there was a sound boat anywhere on the East Coast that I could afford.

I say 'we' because from now on I had a companion on my trips. I had met Pearl at a dance and suggested she should come out with me next day. She came and said nothing when we walked along the river wall at Wivenhoe in the pouring rain and mud to look at the hulk of the wooden brigantine *Cap Pilar*. I stood there, enthralled by the old ship with masts and spars covered in seagull dropping. Pearl still said nothing and I don't think she really understood at this stage quite why anyone should be taking any interest in what was clearly a useless wreck.

A few weeks later I saw the 28ft gaff cutter *Sea Fever* was for sale at £350. The previous summer we had seen her tacking out of Walton Backwaters and Arthur Hunt had pointed out Ron Bayly, who had converted her from a ship's lifeboat and done an expert job. Again we walked along a river wall, this time at Felixstowe Ferry, to look at *Sea Fever*.

Ron Bayly had first sailed *Sea Fever* without an engine, but this was more a credit to his skill that the cutter's ability at sailing. By the time I bought her she had been fitted with a petrol ex-air compressor Stuart Turner with a prop on the quarter. This meant that if you could get the engine to start she turned brilliantly one way and hardly at all the other way. Under sail she would only tack against the wind with a fair tide. The great advantage was that she had a centreboard and for coming over the shallow Deben bar this was a real blessing.

Pearl went off to work in London and I managed to persuade her brother John Bater and Robert Bond to join me in a cruise to Holland. I never had doubts about achieving this, but when Robert came aboard he said.

'Thank goodness the decks are painted yellow, at least the air sea rescue planes will spot us !'

After this vote of confidence, we set sail. Robert's other great contribution to the trip was a large number of old bottles which he had filled with draught beer in the 'Arms' the night before we left. In the tiny cabin we never had found a good storage place for these, so every time we tacked there was the sound below of all these bottles rolling across the floor.

We sailed from the Deben the next morning and headed to where we believed Holland to be. In the excitement of leaving, or perhaps I was not properly awake, I forgot one vital piece of seamanship. After we crossed the Deben bar I stopped the engine, but forgot to lean over the side and stick a cork in the exhaust outlet. As we bobbed gently out into the North Sea, the salt water went up the exhaust pipe and filled the engine. Later when the wind dropped I tried to start the engine, but nothing happened.

This was not a problem as it was beautiful summer weather, but there was hardly a breath of wind. The total crossing time from the Deben to the Schelde, about one hundred and twenty miles, took two and a half days. I think we went the scenic route and after drifting about I had lost any real hope of knowing exactly where we were. Suddenly, on the third day, the wind got up and the North Hinder light vessel appeared in line with the end of the bowsprit. My crew thought that this was part of the plan. I kept quiet and we sailed up to the Belgian light vessel, read the name and then laid a course for the Wester Schelde River. That evening we made our landfall on the flat sandy coast just south of the Schelde. It is probably one of the more disinteresting stretches of European coastline, but I was very excited. At nineteen I had made my first foreign landfall in a boat of my own. At that moment I knew how Christopher Columbus had felt when he hit the Americas, a mixture of sheer relief and real exhilaration.

The plan was to go north though the islands of Zeeland to Rotterdam, but first we spent several days trying to get the engine to work. In the end I sailed from Flushing up the canal across Walcheren Island to Veere on the tidal Veere Gap. We arrived there in the afternoon and walked over to the tidal harbour to see the huge Dutch fishing boats come in. They had single cylinder engines plonking away at a very slow beat. When their crew went down into the fo'c'sle they left their clogs in a neat circle in order of seniority near the scuttle.

Next morning we locked out of Veere and headed out into the tidal channel, *Sea Fever's* air compressor engine sprang into life, but would not push her against the tide. Luckily members of a Dutch yacht club were leaving at the same time and they had hired a tug to tow them through the Veere Gap and out into the Ooste Schelde. The tug collected us up as well and with a string of yachts we were towed to where the tide was favourable. Here we set all sail and ran up inland towards Zierikzee, a lovely red brick Dutch town which looked as if it had remained unchanged from the seventeenth century. In Zierikzee and other small Zeeland towns most of the women over forty still wore the traditional costume. This varied from place to place, but was mostly a long striped skirt, white starched top and white bonnet. Sadly, World War II had destroyed most of the traditional working boats, but considering the damage done only about a decade before, there was very little sign of it.

In the evening we went ashore for a meal. It was then ten guilders to the pound, making The Netherlands very cheap, so we ate well in the cafes and developed a taste for Dutch beer. The flat English bitter under our cabin table was eventually thrown into the North Sea. After our meal we walked back along the canal up to the town and on the bend spotted a circus on a meadow. When we reached the circus they refused to take any money from us. This was because Britain had helped liberate The Netherlands from the occupation of Nazi Germany. We felt slightly embarrassed, as we were all too young to have contributed to Hilter's downfall. It was one of a number of kindnesses shown to us and now the sight of a Dutch flag always makes me feel that friends are at hand.

After Zierikzee we quickly sailed further inland to Willemstad, which was still tidal, where we enjoyed another evening meal in a harbourside cafe. Next, we headed north through the inland waterways towards Rotterdam, where the barge traffic increased in size and number. In the morning it rained hard and I sat alone at *Sea Fever's* tiller peering into the grey ahead trying to pick out the channel buoys. Every so often the cabin hatch was opened and a hand came out with a cup of tea or a thick sandwich.

At Dordrecht, we had to wait for a railway bridge to open, but somehow managed to miss its opening time. It was now afternoon and as we hoped to make Rotterdam before dark we lowered the mast and motored under the bridge. Shortly afterwards our totally inadequate engine gave up for good. I think this was a relief to us all, as hours had been spent trying to coax it back into life, now we gave up altogether and pressed on under sail.

The tide was with us as we beat down the River Maas towards Rotterdam, but progress was slow. There were no yacht havens before Rotterdam and anchoring in the heavy commercial traffic did not seem a good idea. Then we noticed a local yacht being towed by a barge. Why not do the same ? We waved a rope towards the next small barge we saw which at once came over to give us a tow. The barge captain, to my surprise, decided to take the tow rope in the shortest time by cutting close across our bows. We were going much faster than he realised and our bows rode up on his deck and snapped our bowsprit like a match stick against the barge's steel wheelhouse. While we bobbed helplessly in his wake, like a wounded duck, the Dutch skipper rushed out to see if we had damaged his wheelhouse. Fortunately we had not even marked it.

Under tow, with a huge bow wave, we rapidly approached Rotterdam. Here there is an island in the river with a high bridge in the main channel, but to our surprise the barge towed us straight towards the smaller inland bridge and her crew made signs for us to lower our mast. With *Sea Fever* continually rolled in the endless barge wakes, and in order to get the mast down in time, we had to cut the lanyards holding the shrouds. The barge captain finally delivered us to a quay near the Royal Maas Yacht Club and he explained that his boss' office overlooked the main bridge so he had to come through the small bridge. We passed over some guilders and with a cheerful wave he thundered off on his way.

We hauled ourselves into the Royal Maas yacht haven and were greeted by the crew of the Bristol Channel pilot cutter *Hirta* (now *Cornubia*). She had been sailed from Pin Mill by a cheerful bunch of young men, including Roy Bull, all well known in the trendy pubs of Ipswich. Beside our tiny converted ship's lifeboat the *Hirta* seemed more like an ocean liner and I remember being very impressed with a huge coal fired range in the fo'c'sl. The crews of *Hirta* and *Sea Fever* were all full of admiration for the yacht havens in the Netherlands and particularly the Royal Maas. Here we could walk up to the showers and bar, undreamed of luxury to us hardy East Coast types used to muddy hards and very long rows out to our boats. Some thirty years later I returned to the Royal Maas yacht haven again, this time to visit Frits Loomeijer and his Danish wife aboard their motor coaster *Jutland*. The smart yachts of the Royal Maas had given way to the dock becoming a traditional ship haven, but the real surprise was how small it was. The massive new yacht marinas, which had sprung up in both Britain and the Netherlands, now dwarfed this tiny dock.

The passage back to Suffolk under sail was slow, but peaceful. We nailed up the bowsprit and just before dark beat out of the Hook of Holland, dodging the big ships, back

10. After buying this postcard there was a certain amount of relief when we sailed safely out of the Hook of Holland in 1957.

19

into the North Sea. A day was spent going south towards the lighthouse on Walcheren Island, but here we were totally becalmed for twelve hours. The radio was put on the deck and we listened to the pop music on Radio Luxembourg. In the end the wind freshened and we roared into Harwich after nearly two days at sea. The trip took slightly longer than it should have done because I remembered the bargemen taking a short cut inside the Guard Buoy off Harwich. What I had not realised was that they only did this at high tide and we hit the bottom at low tide. I am pleased to say that the Guard Shelf has long since been dredged away and we may have played a small part in this with our centreboard !

The following year four of us set off on another trip. We talked about going to Le Havre, but because of the continual south-westerly we sailed for Ostend. During the winter another-er engine had been fitted and this time I had purchased a piece of machinery that should by rights have had an honoured place in a maritime museum. The new source of power was an Alsia Craig petrol engine, probably dating from around the time of World War I. This beauty was shaped like an upright piano and was just about as useful. The only advice I could get on how to keep it running was the oil bath on the top of the engine had be kept full so that the soft bearing would not overheat. There was little chance of anything over-heating as the dear Alsia Craig seldom ran at all and at the end of the year I sold it to be come a mooring weigh. A task it was ideally suited for.

The North Sea crossing was dramatic, because about halfway across the fresh SW turned into an angry force 6-7 with gusts, we were later told, of up to force 9. I tried to heave-to, but the flax mainsail, an old Royal Naval cutter sail, split in several places. After that we just ran before the gale under bare poles, the windage on the mast gave us steer-age way. While we were on the wave tops, with surf boiling around the stern, there was a view for miles and then we would rush forward down into a deep valley and wonder if the bow would lift again. In the early hours of the morning the wind suddenly dropped leav-ing a huge sea running. *Sea Fever* rolled uncontrollably and spun us around so that the waves smacked into from us all angles. We were exhausted and everything below was soaking wet.

To the east we could see the lights of a ship making for a harbour, but I had no idea how far we had run in twenty-three hours. In fact, it must have been around 120 miles, much farther than I imagined. When we did close with the land and spot a harbour I had no idea where it was. As we approached the wide harbour under our patched sail ·I asked a yachts-man coming out a rather silly question about depth.

A surprised Dutchman replied: 'You know, Scheveningen-ya?'

I dived below to consult our soggy charts and found we were just north of the Hook of Holland, entering a large fishing port and holiday resort. Once under the shelter of the har-bour walls we lost steerage way and I let the anchor go, but clearly we had to get into the inner harbour. The pram dinghy was taken off the foredeck and we rowed ashore trailing 120 fathoms of grass rope, which floated, ashore. Arthur Hunt had told me when I bought *Sea Fever* I would need the grass rope for a kedge anchor. This is how they had entered small ports before World War II. Landing on the beach,our rope end was seized by a small army of young people who towed us up into the harbour with great enthusiasm. Here we were amazed to meet up with the cheerful Pin Mill crowd we had met the year before on the *Hirta,* but this time they were on the smack *Martha Two,* which Roy Bull had bought.

The crew of the *Martha Two* were very proud of being real heroes, as they had entered Scheveningen just as the gale had started and had appeared in the national press and on television. We had missed this brief glory, but were just happy to step on to dry firm land again. Later when sitting in a night club enjoying a steak and listening to a young Dutch girl singing 'Chew, Chew Little Bird', we thought life could not have been better. For the next few days we worked at patching up the sails on the floor of a local chandlery and attempted to get the engine back to life. Roy Bull warned us that we should look out for boys throwing stones at the yachts, but I found the local girls more of a problem. Thanks to the magic attraction of Philip, we always seemed to have a cabin full of them. Several, who were clearly still at school, announced they would be sailing to Belgium with us, while an Italian lady was very keen to come to England and kept appearing and asking if there was a dry place to stow her suitcase.

I was not quite sure how the immigration authorities at Harwich would have viewed the arrival of *Sea Fever* with several young females who all lacked passports. In the end I left Scheveningen suddenly during school and working hours with just my three friends. We sailed south, visited Ostend and then left for Dunkirk planning to take a south-westerly back across the North Sea. Because of *Sea Fever's* poor performance to windward the tide had turned against us just as we got in sight of the cranes of Dunkirk docks. Steadily the wind increased to a force 6 and then the pram dinghy, which had sat on the foredeck happily through the gale, took to sliding off. The worst effect of the great blow was that we started to leak badly. Pumping hard we ran back to Nieuwpoort.

11. The *Sea Fever* sitting on the hard at Nieuwpoort waiting for the tide to drop so that work could begin on the bottom. The man with a horse and board was washing the silt off the hard. 1958.

I began to think that Nieuwpoort was Europe's dullest port which is probably unfair on this little Belgian harbour, but we had a miserable time there. We did not find a welcoming local cafe, as we had done repeatedly in the Netherlands, or friendly sailing people. We put the *Sea Fever* on to a hard and spent most of the night working on the bottom, often in the rain, trying to mend the leak, only to wake next morning and find water over the floorboards again. All the time the wind howled in the rigging and I began to worry about getting home. Finally the leak was stopped and we sailed for Dunkirk again, but at sea the wind switched to a fair south-westerly. I pulled the tiller towards me and headed for Harwich and we had a pleasant sail back. By the time we reached Harwich to clear customs we all felt we had had enough of that trip.

We all go sailing for the good bits, a wonderful fast passage with a fair wind, drifting up the Deben on a peaceful summer's day, but it is the bad bit that stick in the mind. In 1960 *Sea Fever* finally made a successful North Sea cruise, mainly due to a petrol Thornycroft Handibilly engine bought second-hand from Frank Knights on Woodbridge Ferry Quay. We did not use the engine a great deal, but having power to get in and out of harbour and push us through the calm and difficult patches completely changed cruising.

12. *Sea Fever* dwarfed by The Netherland barges in the lock at Flushing. 1960.

13. RS wearily watching the shipping in the Wester Schelde. 1960.

14 . On *Sea Fever* in the canal between Nieuwpoort and Dunkirk, 1960. Left to right Pearl, Jane Smither and RS.

Philip, Jane, Pearl and myself crossed to Ostend in twenty-four hours. Next day we went up the coast, entered the Walcheren Island Canal at Flushing on to the dreamy little town of Veere. This time we turned east with the strong tide into Zandkreek and went through a new lock at Kortgene to reach the tiny tree-lined yacht haven at Goes. The islands of Zeeland were changing rapidly because the rivers were being dammed off from the sea in the massive Delta Plan. The Germans had flooded these islands as they retreated in 1944, and again in 1953 there had been flooding, so the Dutch just wanted to be safe from the sea. Over a decade later we returned to Zeeland in the Thames barge *Redoubtable* and found the area had become a huge inland boating lake.

The four of us on *Sea Fever* in 1960 left Zeeland via the South Beveland Canal into the Wester Schelde and went on up to the city of Antwerp, with its cafes beside cobbled streets. Then we returned to the North Sea coast where plans were ruined by a stiff south-westerly wind. I decided to get as far south as possible for a fair wind across the North Sea, but again we found ourselves hammered by a big head sea off the Belgian coast and ran to Nieuwpoort for shelter. This time I tried a fresh approach and we lowered the mast and went through the Canal de Furnes, following the coast down to Dunkirk.

We found ourselves in a rural backwater, motoring through the flat fields of Flanders. By evening we had reached the French border beside the road and stopped to clear customs. Next morning, a French custom's officer, wearing hob-nailed boots, reluctantly came aboard, clearly horrified that anyone could live on this tiny yacht. He peered down the cabin hatch through the rigging on the deck and said to Jane, the only one amongst us who spoke French, in complete disbelief: 'You live down there mademoiselle !!'

15. Philip Hardiman, Pearl and Jane returning home in *Sea Fever*, 1960. The Kentish Knock lightvessel was in the middle of the Thames Estuary.

Two hours later we were motoring into the outskirts of Dunkirk and stepping back in time. To the north, only a few hours travelling away, in the Wester Schelde, there had been a constant stream of big modern steel diesel-engined barges thundering their way into the heart of Europe. The French barges were mostly wooden, with the cabin amidships, usually the homes of elderly couples, and many of them did not have any power. We passed huge barges being poled along by elderly women and then locked through into the main harbour. Having had an enjoyable cruise, we crossed the North Sea back to Harwich where we collected our pram dinghy.

The weekend before this cruise, Pearl and I had taken *Sea Fever* around to Walton Backwaters. The plan had been to return over the Deben bar about half ebb, which all sounded reasonable, but off Felixstowe Pier a force 6 northerly had sprung up and it took us over two hours to beat the last mile back to the Deben.

We arrived at the entrance to find the channel over the bar a mass of breaking water. Since *Sea Fever* had a centreboard and rudder which could be lifted up this was not a real problem, but once we started the run through breaking water the pram astern kept catching us up and finally   rolled over and acted as a sea anchor. Even with the mainsail full of wind and the engine going flat out, we were unable to make any progress and it was obvious we were soon going to be ashore on the shingle knolls. I cut the pram free and it vanished out to sea as we sailed on with great relief into the calm of the Deben.

While we were in Dunkirk waiting to go to sea we had laid alongside the motor barge *Baiston* of Rochester, which was loaded with wheat for Chelsea. Her mate was a Harwich fishermen called Mudd, who had just joined the barge because the fishing had been bad. He remarked that it was funny that our boat's name was *Sea Fever* because on his last fishing trip out of Harwich he and his brother had picked up a pram with that name on it. Once back in Harwich, I sought out the home of brother Mudd and for ten shillings retrieved my pram dinghy.

This seemed a fair arrangement, but salvaging was then a deep-rooted part of the East Coast tradition. However, real pirates were soon to appear. In 1964 we sailed some six miles off Bawdsey where Radio Caroline, the first of the pirate radio ships, had recently come to anchor. Several men appeared on the deck and were very friendly and we were asked what record we wanted. I shouted Francois Hardy's 'We Are Only Good Friends' and the next morning they played this for 'the little yacht *Sea Fever*'. Many of our friends heard it and pirate radio stations playing pop music quickly became very popular. Three years later there were six pirate radio stations in the Thames Estuary. Returning from a Gaffers' Race, we sailed past three of these radio ships anchored in a line off Walton Naze. This money-making activity was outside the law and there were rumours of London gangs with guns raiding rival stations. Men came on deck, but nobody waved, they just watched us very closely for signs of trouble.

R.S. and Caroline, 1962.

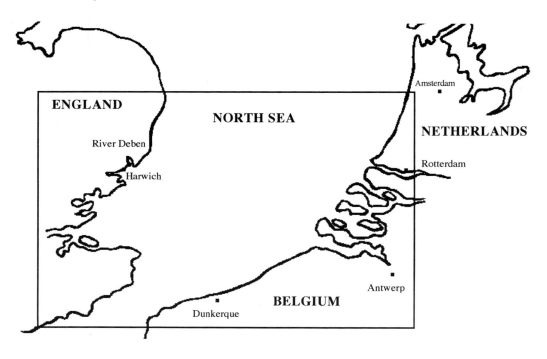

Chapter Three

TOPSAILS OVER THE HORIZON

On a boiling hot morning in July, 1959, Pearl and I left our taxi at the Ten Metre Basin in Copenhagen. At the far end of the dock a 4-masted schooner was discharged of timber, but we were standing outside a ramshackle boatyard and could see a few yacht masts sticking up over the roof. Inside the boat shed we were given a tremendous welcome by Erling Borghegen, an untidy man in a sweat-shirt. Borghegen's business was hiring yachts out to British people and we were shown the Bermudian sloop *Mascot*, which we had chartered.

Fortune really does smile on young love, because this was our honeymoon and we had the most glorious weather for our cruise in The Sound between Denmark and Sweden. Erling Borghegen advised us to make our first sail to the island of Ven where he said 'time has stood still'. We sailed out of Copenhagen to the island of Ven in the middle of The Sound. As we entered the little harbour at Kyrkbacken, the first feature I noticed was two privies on the harbour wall, which emptied straight into the clear blue water. Ven was indeed an island which was still part of the nineteenth century. This was also our first attempt at mooring in a tideless harbour, by dropping the anchor over the stern and going bows-on to the quay.

I had wanted to go to Denmark because wooden sailing vessels were still trading there. I had hoped to photograph them, but my lack of skill and a poor quality camera produced nothing of interest. However there were wooden traders everywhere. Two big black wooden ketches, jagt-built galeses with their flat sloping Marstal sterns, were laid up for sale in Kyrkbacken and at every harbour we visited there were Baltic traders going about their normal work.

16. Kyrkbacken on the Swedish island of Ven, 1959.

As we sailed north, the Sound became increasingly narrow, until off Elsinore Castle there were only three miles between Denmark and Sweden. All the large shipping going between the North Sea and the Baltic funnelled through The Sound and it was alive with little Baltic schooners, ketches and trading sloops, all with their diesel engines thumping away. We headed for the Swedish port of Helsingborg and here there were steel ketches loading wheat. These were in fact former Dutch herring loggers which had been convert- ed for cargo carrying. At that time Sweden and Denmark had poor road systems and also few of the small islands had been connected by road bridges, so this gave plenty of inter- island work for these schooners and ketches.

Our roughest and shortest trip was the three miles across The Sound from Helsingborg to Helsingor, back on the Danish side. A stiff northerly breeze was blowing, pushing a lively sea down from the Kattegat and it was a full-time job dodging the shipping bound through The Sound. It was a relief to get under the shelter of the point and see the impres- sive green roof and spires of Elsinore Castle. Since the Kattegat did not seem very wel- coming, we headed back south down The Sound past the high white chalk cliff of Stevns Klint and into the open Baltic or as the Danes called it, the Ostersoen, or east sea.

On the *Mascot* cruise we met another of Borghegen's boats with a family from Manchester, who had managed to run ashore in the Praesto Fjord. Going ashore in tidal waters is bad enough, but in the tideless Baltic this family had come to a total standstill

17. Pearl on the Danish yacht *Mascot* at Helsingborg, 1959.

and had hired a fishing boat to drag them off. I thought of their misfortune as we crossed Faskse Bay on a misty day and approached the Bogestrom, part of a narrow channel which separates Zealand from the islands to the south. We were still some way off the land but when I looked over the side down into the clear water, I saw we were sailing at speed over huge smooth white stones. We were not in the channel and, thanks to Mr Borghegen's compass of uncertain age, we were much too far to the west. Tacking to the east we picked up the shipping moving through the clearly marked Bogestrom.

We then visited Nyord, another of the tiny islands where time had stood still, where the only contact with outside world was via a very rickety jetty. The water was very shallow here, but we continued up another very narrow channel to Stage and then finally the town of Vordingborg. This was a lovely area with green fields coming down to water's edge, but all very shallow water and it was a relief to go back through the Bogestrom into the deeper water. We stopped at Rodvig going back north. There were two trading sloops here, one was for sale and another discharging.

The very hot weather in the Sound created a final surprise for us. This was after we had stopped at Dragor, where we walked through old streets with their single storey half-timbered houses lined with hollyhocks. By this time, the *Mascot's* engine had given up, and one got the feeling Mr Borghegen ran his fleet on a very tight budget. As I prepared to sail away from the quay, the Harbour Master arrived and appeared to be ordering us not to move, but I pretended not to understand and sailed away from the quay without any problems to start the short hop back to Copenhagen. The Harbour Master was still shouting in Danish as we happily cleared the harbour and perhaps it was his wrath which conjured up a water spout. It appeared just to the east of us and to my relief it moved rapidly off to the north. Borghegen was as cheerful as ever when we got back to the Ten Meter Basin and he was very excited about the water spout. 'Old men', he told us, 'who have been at sea all their lives, have never seen one here before.'

Borghegen was neither surprised nor angry that his yacht should have been returned with an engine and several other features that had failed to work. Years later I tried to find him and his yacht yard, but found no trace of them. I hope he had a happy retirement.

It was nearly twenty years before we returned to the Baltic again. This time, with our family, we joined Peter Baker on his 68ft galease *I.P.Thorsoe* at Marstal, once a great schooner-owning port, on the Island of Aero. We sailed north and, even in the channel running along the low island of Langeland, we could look overboard and see the huge smooth stones on the sea bed. We wound close between the islands of Turo and Taasing to the little yard then run by Michael Kiersgaard at Troense. Old sea captains came down from their homes to see the black ketch arrive.

The *I.P. Thorsoe* had been brought back to her native land for some repairs, but by then few of her type remained. When road bridges had been built to link most of these islands, hundreds of Baltic traders came on the market. A few stayed in Denmark, but most were sold as yachts to owners in western Europe and America. Bought cheaply, they became the vehicle for many hoping to make romantic world voyages. However, they had very short careers in their new role as adventure ships, and within a decade the bones of unfortunate Baltic traders decorated harbours all over the world. All that remains of *I.P. Thorsoe* is a rotting hulk in the mud above Brightlingsea. She looked happier in her rightful home amongst the islands of Denmark's Zealand.

Most of the craft that I had sailed on were old barges and yachts, where things were always 'carrying away', and you had to soldier on. So, it was a welcome relief in 1962 when I was asked to crew on the brand new ocean racer *Giselle of Iken,* the first fibreglass yacht based on the Deben and I think she must have been one of the first on the East Coast.

We were all very excited about this new fibreglass material, but it was a little disconcerting to be able to see the water through the hull. The *Giselle* was owned by George Gooderham senior, but Michael Spear, who had a lot of ocean-racing experience and even greater skills at getting on with everyone, was the unofficial skipper. The big test against all the wooden and steel ocean racers was the Hook of Holland Race, over a Z course across the North Sea.

At the North Hinder light vessel we turned to beat back across the North Sea to Smith's Knoll. My own simple passage-making instinct began to arouse in me - why not just go on to Ostend and have a sociable meal ashore? Instead, we had a hard beat back all the way to the other side of the North Sea. This American-designed centreboard yawl was joy to sail to windward in a seaway, but all the electrics packed up and we could not even make a cup of tea. Being at the wheel of *Giselle* as she sliced through the cold grey seas with spray thrown up over the genny was an exhilarating experience, but my heart was not in it and my stomach certainly was not.

I forget what position we finished in the race, but only remember a mad piece of motoring up the North Sea Waterway to the Royal Maas Yacht Club for a quick party, before leaving at once to motor back home across the North Sea. Up until this time I suppose I had been part of the normal leisure-sailing scene, but from this point on I became part of a new era of people who sailed only traditional working craft.

Most traditional craft at that time were really at the end of their lives, worn out by decades of work. We used to go and sail with Chris Gurteen on the West Mersea smack *Edith*, a craft which handled beautifully, but the mainsail had been made in 1927 and below the cabin floor the frames had rotted away where they came out of the cement ballast. Worse still was a little smack called *Marita*, which I helped Gordon Hardy sail while he was delivering her from Maldon to Melton. When we stepped aboard the water was above the cabin floor and we had to pump most of the time, but even worse, all the gear was rotten. We had to keep tying up sheets and as we tacked up the Deben a throat halliard broke, the mainsail came crashing down and we ploughed up the mud.

At that time nobody had thought seriously about rebuilding traditional craft. They were bought cheaply, patched up to keep them sailing for a few more years and then abandoned in some lonely creek. Both *Edith* and *Marita* have long gone, as have hundreds, probably thousands, of similar craft around the coast of Britain. It was a great dream to see if the clock could be put back and we could once again see these handsome craft sailing as they had in their halcyon days, before World War I.

Late in September 1961, Pearl and I sailed *Sea Fever* down the Essex coast and on the River Blackwater we met up with Peter Light. He had bought the 44ft Tollesbury smack *Sallie* and that summer was running charter trips in her from the Mill Beach at Heybridge. He explained that because the upper Blackwater dried out at low tide, few yachtsmen were interested in keeping boats there. The Hythe Quay at Maldon had, by tradition, provided free berthing for barges between freights so people began buying them out of trade and bringing them to the Hythe.

The following summer, we returned to Maldon to see a fleet of sailing barges, lead by *Marjorie* skippered by Peter, sweep around Herring Point up to their race finish off the Promenade. This was first of a new series of races for barges sailed for pleasure. Around Maldon a hard band of traditionalists, most of them with some connection with the last

18. *Sea Fever* heading up the River Colne at the finish of the 1965 East Coast Old Gaffers Race. Ian Clarke and Colin Shannon are on the foredeck.

barges working under sail, came up with a new approach. They started rebuilding old boats and keeping alive the art of sailing them.

The East Coast traditional boat revival movement took another step forward the following spring, when six of us met in John Scarlett's front room at 70B Fambridge Road, Maldon, and agreed to hold a race solely for gaff-rigged boats. We took the name, the Old Gaffers' Race, from an event being held on the south coast. The idea for an East Coast race had come about after a dispute following a Maldon smack race. Roy Clarkson, who owned the smack *Fly,* had won the Maldon Smack Race, but since he had a new suit of sails other smack owners, who only had old sails, said this was unfair and not in the spirit of the event. Roy said he would start his own race.

Us hardened East Coast cruising types said we would have nothing to do with racing around buoys like the Sunday yachtsmen. No, we would have a proper passage race, Osea Island to Harwich, but on the appointed day there was no wind. Most gave up the struggle near Colne Point and we, in *Sea Fever,* motored into Harwich ahead of the fleet. Going into the Pier Hotel the manager was delighted to see us.

'You're late !' he cried in despair ' I have another do in an hour. Sit down!' The three of us sat down in the dining room and suddenly the door burst open and the waitress started serve over a hundred sausage suppers. We retreated at speed and were delighted to see the *Fly* motoring in with John and Roy aboard. We all returned to the Pier Hotel and the sausage supper started arriving again. In the moonlight the cutter *Corista* sailed up into Harwich Harbour, and it was a great relief when her crew and those from *Fanny, Edith* and others came and helped out with the sausage mountain!

As a race, that first event was a flop, but it was the spark which started the forest fire of enthusiasm for the gaff rig. We linked up with the south coast that autumn to form the Old Gaffers' Association and after about a decade we turned the tide and brought the gaff rig back into fashion. Publicity given to the races gave respectability to second-hand boats and re-introduced topsails to the gaff rig.

John Scarlett did tremendous work as the first OGA secretary and was still there when I became President in 1983, but sadly he died shortly afterwards. The aim was then to open up the Association, but there was a lot of soul-searching about which way the OGA should go. Some wanted to change the 'silly name' and many wanted it to be just for 'real gaffers', built before World War I. Many new gaff classes and gaff boats were being built and the way forward seemed to be to let in every gaff craft, whatever its age.

19. In the 1968 East Coast Old Gaffers' Race, Ian Clarke and Tony Winter rigged up six sails, but *Sea Fever* still did not sail much faster! (*Yachting Monthly*)

The OGA was like a snowball rolling down a hill, bits kept dropping off, but the main theme kept getting larger. I was a keen promoter of gaff boats and it was heartening to see the whole association expanding. We travelled all over Britain, and indeed much of western Europe and further afield ,with this aim. In Devon I found myself at the helm of Essex smack *Shamrock* in the Dartmouth OGA Race, at Flensburg on a cold autumn night I officially re-launched the Danish fish boat *Havet* in the dark. Far away down on the south coast of Tasmania we took part in the Royal Hobart Regatta, a very relaxed event, sailing on the 33ft topsail schooner *Delphia* which John Kennedy had built to transport wool from Three Hummock Island back to northern Tasmania. There are many wonderful sailing areas in Europe, but here you are never far away from crowds of yachts. On the Delaware River, with mountains rising above the little city of Hobart, just a little group of boats sailed on an otherwise deserted river.

Very sadly, I lost contact with *Sea Fever*. By that time we had three children and needed a bigger boat, so we sold her. For a few years she remained based on the Deben, then a young American sailed her away. I never saw, or heard of her, again. She was the centre of my life for thirteen years and it was like losing track of a member of the family.

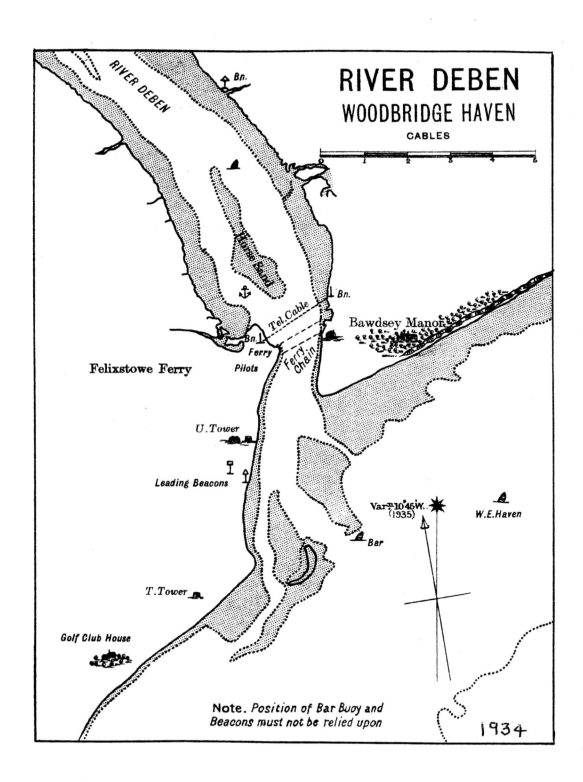

RIVER DEBEN
WOODBRIDGE HAVEN
CABLES

RIVER DEBEN

Bn.

Horse Sand

Tel.Cable

Bn.

Bn.

Ferry

Ferry Chain

Bawdsey Manor

Felixstowe Ferry

Pilots

U. Tower

Leading Beacons

Var⁴ 10°45'W.
(1935)

W.E. Haven

Bar

T. Tower

Golf Club House

Note. *Position of Bar Buoy and Beacons must not be relied upon*

1934

Chapter Four

BE PREPARED WITH A LUCKY HORSE SHOE

L'Atalanta changed my life. As a boy, I had first seen this 35ft black Scandinavian gaff cutter on a mooring off Ramsholt Dock. I rowed around her several times and thought that one day I would like to own a boat like that. In 1969 she came on the market at £2400, a sum of money I could not raise. I suppose that was the same price as an average house then and it was the first time that I fully realised that it was impossible to achieve a dream without hard cash.

I was unable to buy *L'Atalanta,* but a year later I heard that her new owner, Colin Wade, wanted a quick sale. I dropped everything and headed for Great Yarmouth to find a rather battered *L'Atalanta* lying at the old maltings quay at Gorleston. Sitting in the cabin we agreed £1400 (cash) and since Colin was sad to sell her, and as he had not used her very much, I suggested that he and his friends should crew her back to the Deben. However, he did not tell me that they were going to a party the night before.

I wanted to take the whole of the favourable flood tide down the coast to the Deben, but by the time Colin and his friends arrived, much of the valuable tide had gone. During her stay at Gorleston *L'Atalanta* had got her stern up under a pier which smashed down the rail, so there was nowhere to sheet the mainsail. I planned to get her back to the Deben for the repairs and since she had a good diesel engine it did not seem a problem. In spite of a head wind, all went well to start with because we were under the shelter of the land. There was a bit of fun in the tide race off Lowestoft when the boom broke free, almost knocking two girls (who they had met at the party) overboard. Shortly after this we began to meet a head sea and most of the crew became seasick. As I sat in the wheel shelter with Colin, he told me about his rise and fall as a builder, and I hoped the driving spray would not soak through my clothes and wet the bundles of notes in my pocket with which I intended to buy the boat.

Rounding Orfordness, we began to meet the full force of the wind, but then off Shingle Street the tide turned against us. As so often happens when the tide turns, the weather altered and in this case a moderate breeze suddenly became a young gale. We only had to make three miles to the Deben entrance, but the wind increased to force 7 and it rained so hard that it seemed to flatten the seas. *L'Atalanta* was a heavily-built craft of the pilot cutter type. In the shallow waters a steep sea quickly built up. The black cutter was flung around like a dinghy, but the diesel engine kept pushing her forward. As the bows hit each wave, a solid wall of spray rose briefly into the air and then flew on to the deck and came rushing aft to where we sat in the wheel shelter.

My agreement with Colin had been that he would fill up the diesel tanks and as we bashed past Boathouse Point, Bawdsey he broke the news that this had not been done and would it make any difference? My heart sank. We were at sea in a gale, close to the shore, in a craft in which we could not set sails and which was rapidly running out of diesel. We arrived off the Deben entrance an hour and three-quarters after high water. Close under the land the sea was smoother, but the ebb rushing over the bar made the channel a mass of breaking water.

Although the surf over the shingle bar looked horrendous, I hoped there was still enough

20. *L'Atalanta* and *Sea Fever* ashore for a scrub. Very different craft. 1973.

water in the channel. Certain that the engine would stop at any moment, I lined up the two metes, the posts roughly marking the channel over the bar, and turned for the breaking water. Water was everywhere and once a wave broke over the stern, but we got in over the bar all right and fought the ebb for a few more minutes up to Bawdsey Ferry where the engine suddenly died and we let the anchor go.

Of course we had good luck, but then this black cutter carried her own luck with her. Nailed on the inside of a stem post was a lucky horse shoe. Following the custom of all Scandinavian work boats it was, to British eyes, the wrong way up. It seemed to have been there since she was built, mostly of oak with iron fastenings as the Swedish 'toll jakt' (custom cutter) *Ran* in 1904 by Gustafsson at Landskrona. The name *Ran* came from a Norse goddess who lived at the bottom of the sea and caught drowned sailors in a net. Eight owners and seven name changes later she was *L'Atalanta*. I would have given her the original name back, but it took several years to trace her full history. By then we had got used to *L'Atalanta,* a name none of us could ever pronounce, which seems to have originated from a pre-war French film.

Amazingly, the sons of the man who had built her nearly seventy years before were still alive in the early 1970s. They were referred to in Sweden as the 'nice old Gustafsson Brothers' and they remembered all the cutters their father had built. They said that because she was a government job the best material was used. Although she had the typical Scandinavian round stern and out door rudder, just as the Copenhagen *Mascot* had, the deep bow had probably been inspired by English custom cutters.

The *Ran* had gone into service at Torekov, but the custom's men said she was too big so

Gustafsson built a smaller cutter, the *Kryess*, on the same lines. When I got to know *L'Atalanta* better I suspected that the custom's men found her unhandy for beating into small harbours, the deep forefoot made her very slow at tacking. In 1912 the *Ran* was sold as a yacht and was eventually bought by Bertil Priesler of Landskrona. He spent a fortune on her and in fact seems to have run into money troubles over his yachting expenses. Bertil went afloat wearing a proper reefer jacket and yachtsman's peaked cap and in 1926 ripped out the gaff rig, making her one of the first Bermudian yachts in Sweden. This was a total flop because she would not sail at all until the bowsprit was restored.

In 1933 Gunnar Malmquist bought the cutter, converted her back to a gaff cutter and fitted a wheel shelter, as he and a party of army officers intended to sail her round the world. I doubt if that voyage was ever completed because the only evidence I can find over the next year is a postcard of her sailing into Ramsgate, and then she came on the British register owned at Cowes. When she arrived at Woodbridge in 1937 she still had the seal-skin sleeping bags from the round the world voyage project and even when I bought her the blocks and spars were too large for the sail area.

Actually her sail area had steadily been reduced as the engine size increased. I was very disappointed with the way she sailed and over the next twenty-three years was constantly coming up with improvements. Hours were spent in Jim Lawrence's sail loft working out new sail plans and she did improve. Basically the length of bowsprit and boom were increased, but her own real 'secret weapon' was a huge lightweight headsail from the bowsprit end to the top of the pole mast. When this was set she took off, but it needed a block and tackle and several strong crewmen to sheet it in.

I have never been interested in racing, but the races for gaff boats have forced the forgotten skills of handling a gaff craft to be revived. *L'Atalanta's* modest racing successes were due to the big jib and her long keel length which made her fast down-wind. Once in 1974 we sailed from the Deben to Greenhithe in ten hours, carrying the flood tide most of the way into the Thames and then next day in a run up river won the gaff class in the second Thames Smack and Barge Race to Greenwich. Another time, in 1983, we won the work-boat class in the first Stour Gaffers' Race. It was blowing NE force 4-6 and running with the big jib and topsail set we ran from Harwich Pound to Mistley in an hour and must have been going over the ground at eight knots.

There seems to be a law of the sea which says that if things start to go right the whole trip will be a success, but if a tide is missed or some quite small piece of gear carries away this has a knock-on effect and the trip can slowly turn into a disaster. It was no wonder that the old sailing ship men were so superstitious. If the mysterious and totally unforgiving gods of the sea were offended then they would bring bad luck on you.

There is no room for mistakes when crossing the Deben bar. The winter gales move thousands and thousands of tonnes of shingle and create different shaped knolls with a new main channel over the bar. Every spring when we first cross the Deben bar, and the Shingle Street one four miles to the north into the River Ore, it is like finding a new river. In the period of well nearly fifty years, since I first went over the Deben bar in the *Lora* and then *Sea Fever*, the channel has moved steadily to the south. The shingle point on the south-west shore has gone and the knolls form a line so that the channel over the bar was, in 1998, in front of the golf clubhouse. There are two metes ashore to line up for the channel, but these posts are only moved periodically. Even in the summer the channel is steadily moving. Sometimes it is possible to pick out the channel by watching the way the water surface behaves, providing you can see the entrance.

21. *L'Atalanta* following the Pin Mill barge race. Bob More on deck, 1973. (*Alf Pyner*)

22. *L'Atalanta* coming up the River Blackwater to the finish of the 1984 East Coast Old Gaffers' Races off Stone Sailing Club. (*Basil Emmerson*)

23. The winners of a Gaffers' race on *L'Atalanta's* deck at Manningtree. Jonathan, third from right, was there with the *Pet* and RS on the right, 1983.

Once in *Sea Fever* in a low sea mist we hoisted someone up the mast and they could pick out the land and con us in over the bar. Another time in *L'Atalanta* I found the way back from West Mersea in fog, but could not find the bar buoy. A fishing boat passed across our bow and the wheelhouse opened and a voice shouted 'follow us if you like, we are just coming into the channel'. I spun the wheel and followed the fishing boat. Suddenly the fishing boat swung around as it ran spectacularly aground on a shingle knoll on a falling tide. I went hard astern, the fishing boat was lost in the fog, but in the confusion I found the bar buoy and slowly crept in over the bar.

In *L'Atalanta* I once tried going out at half ebb tide, got out of the channel and grounded. The impact on hitting the hard shingle sent a horrible shudder through the boat. Worse still, for weeks afterwards my sailing friends came up to me beaming, saying ' I hear you've been on the bar!' Bad news travels very fast.

In *L'Atalanta* I had a regular crew and expert rope worker in Bill Coke who was steeped in the superstitions of the sea. He taught us that you could 'buy wind' by throwing a coin into the sea in the direction you wanted the wind to come from, but only a small coin so that you did not get too much wind. Bill joined us as he was recovering from losing one leg. He had been bosun on the Hudson's Bay seventeenth century replica *Nonsuch,* when sailing up the Thames her boat had got caught in some lighters. Bill went to free it and got the rope around his leg, which tightened and took off his foot. Later more of the leg had to be removed. His first trip with us was a lively Old Gaffers' Race and Bill's new artificial leg came off and was washing around on the lee deck while he determinedly hopped around the foredeck sorting out sails. He loved sailing and the sea and said coming with us restored his confidence.

Bill had the true old sailor's ability of accepting the situation as it was and just getting on with the work. He was brilliant at the wheel and could steer a very straight course and sat there happily yarning about all his sailing days. Once in the 1930s he had sailed around the world in a converted zulu, a type of Scottish fishing lugger. They went into Weymouth to say their farewells and sailing out they knocked a car off the quay with their bowsprit.

24. RS at the wheel of *L'Atalanta* on the run down the River Blackwater in the East Coast Old Gaffers' Race, 1979.

25. Sailing in the Black Stakes Reach off the Deben on *L'Atalanta*. RS, Pearl and Bill Coke about 1976. *(Hugh Perks)*

26. Joanna, Jonathan, Caroline and Pearl in *L'Atalanta's* cabin in 1980. We anchored at Orford for the night on a trip between Ramsholt and Snape.

This was of course in the days when bowsprits were very large and cars were very small. During World War II the Royal Navy had seen fit to send Bill out to the eastern Mediterranean on scouting missions in command of Levantine schooners. To him this was more like an extra piece of sailing. Sadly, he was drowned on the Norfolk Broads, a little ironic because he went there thinking it was a safe place to sail in his old age.

A regular crew is a blessing to any craft and our most long-standing crew is Bob More, a careful man who stows everything neatly and never breaks the gear. I first met Bob in 1971 when we were going away for a trip on the barge *Convoy* with Richard Duke to Sittingbourne. It was raining and Bob was wearing a new oilskin jacket as we stood waiting on Pin Mill Hard under the shelter of *Convoy's* bow. In 1997, as we beat the *Crangon* back from Maritime Ipswich, it came on to rain in the River Orwell and out came the same, slightly patched oilskins.

Good luck is important to any ship, but when I sailed the Baltic three-masted topsail schooner *Charlotte Rhodes* in 1975 she still had a lucky horseshoe in the bow, but was running short of her Nordic good fortune. She had been chartered for a sales promotion voyage around Britain. I was due to join her at Inverness, but arrived to find the schooner was nowhere in sight. Over the next three days I was kept in touch by phone with the promotion office in London to learn of the schooner's battering voyage up the east coast of Scotland against a series of gales. Finally to my delight the message came that she was just locking into the Caledonian Canal.

No-one took much notice when I dropped my bags on the deck and scrabbled aboard. The truth was that they were having rather a tough voyage and many of the people invited to join her had left, far from happy about the experience. The schooner had been hired because of her fame in the television series 'Onedin Line', but she had no real accommodation. We slept on mattresses thrown on the hold floor and tried to find places where the deck didn't leak.

For the next two days it rained hard for most of the time and we motored through the Great Glen with the spectaclar mountains of the Scottish Highlands rising on either side. I spent the whole time as we crossed Loch Ness with my camera at hand, just in case we spotted the monster. Jilly Cooper, now a renowned novelist, but then making a name as a *Sunday Times* columnist, and her husband Leo also joined us and were very disappointed. They had expected the grand panelled cabins which had appeared in the 'Onedin Line' series to be on the ship. In fact these had been studio mock-ups, and the Coopers were allotted a sort of rabbit-hutch type cabin at the forward end of the hold. The only real cabin was the one aft, firmly occupied by the skipper owner.

I suspect Jilly Cooper did not find that trip a very fruitful source of material. One evening, after sitting around the table when everyone was relaxing and starting to tell stories Jilly suddenly began her research by asking: 'You are all men on here, you have been away from your women for weeks, how do you manage without sex?'

There was a total silence at the cabin table, the question remained unanswered and for the rest of the time all the crew kept out of her way. She was clearly puzzled by their embarrassment at her question.

When we locked out of the canal at Fort William it was still raining and also blowing a gale. The crew of four men, from the schooner's home port of Dartmouth, said they were not looking forward to the sea passage because the ship was showing definite signs of age. The Coopers and the publicity men suddenly realised they had pressing business back in London and a taxi was summoned. I stayed, trusting to the lucky horse shoe in the bow.

27. The clipper-built Baltic three-masted topsail schooner *Charlotte Rhodes.*

When the weather cleared a little we sailed down Loch Linnhe and the North Channel and down towards Swansea. We spotted the three-masted topsail schooner *Captain Scott* running up to Fort William, a tiny white speck dwarfed by the towering cliffs of Mull.

The *Charlotte Rhodes* was basically a good seaboat. Back in her land of origin, Denmark, she would have been called 'clipper built' because she had a curved bow and a counter stern. For her first twenty years after being built at Svendborg by Ring Andersen in 1903, she had been in the Newfoundland salted cod trade. She did seem very small to have carried cargoes across the North Atlantic, but this had once been normal work for vessels from the west coast of Britain and Denmark. My old mentor Arthur Hunt had been a seaman in about 1907 in the three-masted topsail schooner *Alert,* a Newfoundland trader, and saw nothing unusual about a 103ft deeply-laden schooner sailing across the Western Ocean.

Leaving the shelter of the Mull, we came out into the open sea and sailed steadily past the Isle of Colonsay. Huge dark blue seas were rolling in and bursting in a cloud of spray on the outlying rocks of Colonsay. In the late afternoon, just before it got dark, the rain cleared for a while and the sun lit up the faraway hills of Islay. By midday the following day we were through the North Channel and the wind was increasing. There was talk of going into Stranraer but that port was to windward. By midday the wind had increased and was gusting at force 10.

The *Charlotte Rhodes* had been rigged out again after a long period as the motor ship *Meta Jan* and was really under-canvassed. Under mizzen, gaff foresail and inner jib she handled well in the gale, but the strain of the pounding was beginning to tell. The caulking between the planking was working free and the hull began to leak. In nautical circles this is known as 'making water' while land people, more aware of the dangers, call it sinking. The crew all worked hard clearing the motor pumps and keeping the huge Danish hand pump going. Down in the hold many of our belongings were washing around in a

28. Aboard the three-masted topsail schooner *Charlotte Rhodes* in the North Channel, 1975.

great wall of dirty brown water which rolled from side to side. It became increasingly obvious, that in spite of the pumps, the water in the hold was increasing.

We turned back to run for Belfast Lough and for four hours battled against the fury of the Irish Sea, then between rain showers we saw the coast of Northern Ireland. I took turns with the Captain at the wheel, but most of the time he was on the radio. His request for assistance was picked up by a new supertanker in the Lough and not long afterwards the Donaghadee lifeboat appeared, riding over the sea beside us. But luck was on our side because on a fresh tack she didn't leak, obviously the place where caulking had come out was above the waterline. There was a look of confidence on the face of Pete Lucas, the mate who everyone relied on, when he appeared on deck and said at last the pumps were finally gaining on the water in the hold.

When the pilot for Belfast Lough came aboard I was alone at the wheel. He gave a course and casually asked what my position was on the ship. I replied I was a passenger and he retorted 'what kind of ship comes here sinking with a passenger at the wheel!'

The skipper-owner was very worried that the event would bring the schooner bad publicity. Indeed he was right, the *Charlotte Rhodes'* fame through the 'Onedin Line' series meant that the schooner's plight off the coast of Northern Ireland was widely reported. Later I learned from Cliff Hawkins that he had been sitting at home in faraway Auckland, New Zealand hearing of the *Charlotte Rhodes'* troubles. We knew nothing of this as the schooner eventually crept up a quay in the centre of the troubled city of Belfast at about midnight. Nearby was the steel schooner *Result,* formerly a North Devon trader, waiting to be taken inland to a museum. The *Charlotte Rhodes'* days at sea were also running out. After going into dry-dock she returned to Devon and was then sold to an owner in Amsterdam to join the growing Dutch inland sea charter fleet. But this was not to be, she was impounded by the city and while in a dock caught on fire, probably caused by homeless people living aboard, and was burnt out to the waterline. Her luck finally ran out.

29. The topsail schooner *Charlotte Rhodes* in the Irish Sea, 1975.

Chapter Five

STRONG TIDES IN GREAT ESTUARIES

The start of the Humber Barge Race off Victoria Pier, Hull in 1994 was in a light September breeze. Aboard the 61ft Sheffield-size keel, skipper Colin Screeton and his loyal crew of staunch Humbersiders were playing it cool and sailing as slowly as possible. The turning mark was just above the Humber Bridge, but with the tide still flooding, if we got there too soon the keel would be swept far up river. It was not so much a race as a test of seamanship on the swirling brown waters of the Humber.

Above the Humber Bridge all five entrants beat around trying not to be swept past the Floating Light turning mark. The bluff-bowed steel *Comrade,* with her two square sails set on a single mast, behaved beautifully, but there was never any suggestion that she could make any progress against the tide. In the late afternoon, just as the ebb started, the wind increased rapidly to an easterly gale bringing heavy rain sweeping into the Humber. The sails were stowed and the keel's engine was just about able to push her back to Hull.

The Humber off Hull is some two miles wide and carries the silt-laden water coming from the rivers of the English East Midlands. This was the first time I had been on the great estuary for nearly forty years. The tides were just as formidable as when we used to arrive with wheat on the *Will Everard* in 1955, but everything else had changed. The last Humber keels and sloops had given up using sails about 1938, so I never expected to see these craft under sail. Yet I returned over half a century later to see the traditional craft of the Humber under sail, even if it was only for pleasure. There were the keels *Comrade* and

30. Colin Screeton, left, and the crew of the Humber keel *Comrade,* 1994.

June, the Humber sloop *Amy Howson* (which had the same hull shape as the keel, but a gaff rig) and even the ketch billyboy *Audrey* sailing. On land the story was the other way around. While nearly forty years before I had once walked through two miles of docks and wharves full of coasters and deep sea trawlers, incredibly this whole shipping scene had completely vanished. Only one trawler was left at Hull and most of the docks were empty and lined with derelict warehouses.

I had been fascinated by the waterfront at Hull in the mid-fifties, particularly with the deep water trawlers with their long thin funnels and high bows for the mountainous seas around Iceland. In the *Will Everard's* fo'c'sle Cyril and Nobby had not rated Hull very highly.

Cyril had explained 'We will soon be going down the Channel to the Isle of Wight and Exeter, that is really beautiful down there. We meet these old schooners with high bulwarks and large crews of old men, you would like that'.

I did not go with them, but returned home. Shortly afterwards there was a report of their problems in the newspaper. They had sailed south, but been caught in a gale off Dungeness. The sails had been blown away (they were just old ones from other barges) and worse still, the engine packed up. Paddy O'Donnell, Cyril and Nobby were taken off by a lifeboat. The barge had drifted for some time before being picked up by French fishermen. She had sunk the first French trawler which went alongside but eventually they had towed her into a port.

31. On the Humber keel *Comrade* sailing towards the Humber Bridge, 1994.

In the autumn of 1957 I set out to try and find the last of the West Country vessels. I read in *Sea Breezes* reports about a fleet of motor schooners and ketches, based around Appledore in north Devon, which were still trading. I did not get to Appledore, but I reached Gloucester Dock, which was full of motor barges. The high brick warehouses all around made it seem like a smaller version of the London docks. Totally unimpressed, I went further west to Pill, a little village on the River Avon just below Bristol. I knew this had been the home of the pilot cutters, but there were just a few yachts sitting in the grey Avon mud. The members of the local yacht club were very friendly and they showed me the lone pilot cutter, but she had been heavily altered to become a yacht of the inter-war period. I lost heart, besides travel was expensive, and returned home. I had a feeling that I had missed seeing traditional sailing vessels of the west of England.

In 1969 I returned west to Bristol, but this time with the local maritime artist Peter Stuckey as my guide. He proudly showed me a model of the pilot cutter *Marguerite T* in the Bristol City Museum, all there was to show in the area of these famous craft. This time I got to Appledore, but the only vessel there was the schooner *Kathleen & May,* which was laid up on the mud above the town. The West Country fleet of trading vessels had gone for ever.

In 1997 I visited Boscastle on the north Cornish coast. The harbour is just a gap in the cliffs and, in heavy rain, I watched a huge sea roaring into this little basin. It must have been a very difficult place for sailing traders of the West Country to come in loaded with coal. When we visited Bude, just up the coast, it was a calm day, but a huge ground swell was rolling in smashing against the rocky island in front of the harbour. To try and find out how a sailing vessel had operated on this inhospitable coast I sought out Peter Herbert, who seemed be the last man around who had been master of West Country vessels. His fame in Bude rested on his successful campaign to stop the council filling in the Bude Canal!

Peter had left Bude and moved up to Northam. He was living in a bungalow with the front room walls decorated with paintings of schooners. From his front window there was a good view of the shipping going over the Appledore Bar. Peter could remember that the first year he went to sea, in 1943, he had watched nine vessels, North Devon schooners and ketches, coming over the Appledore Bar when they came home for Christmas.

Peter had grown up in Bude and remembered, with great sadness, the loss of the Bude ketch *Ceres* in 1936, which was returning home to lay up for the winter and ran ashore in a fog and broke up. A great blow to everyone locally because she had become famous as the oldest British coasting vessel. The little ketch had been built in 1811 and had traded from Bude since 1826. Most of that time she was owned and sailed by the Pethericks and they replaced her with the steel motor ketch *Traly* which loaded 165 tons and traded until after World War II.

Peter Herbert has a great love for ships and buying those which take his fancy. He started with the Appledore ketch *Emma Louise*, but did not get her back to sea. In 1955 he bought the *Agnes,* which was the smallest ketch trading. Officially she had been built in Bude in 1904, but actually she was a far older vessel. The builders had got the hulk of the *Lady Acland,* which had been built at Bude in 1835, and lengthened her. Peter had two profitable years trading the *Agnes*, which loaded 107 tons, with any freight that was offered. He took coal down to the Hayle River and discharged drums of oil on the beach at Lundy Island.

Most of the trade then was grain from the ports in South Wales or coal from Lydney down to the West Country ports. After the *Agnes* Peter had the steel ketch *Mary Stewart,* which loaded 120 tons, and the *Emily Barratt* which loaded 115 tons.

Because of his experience in West Country vessels, Peter became master of the *Redoubtable*, a big wooden spritsail barge which George Gooderham operated in charter work from Snape, in 1976. The *Redoubtable* was one of the largest wooden spritsail barges built, 89ft long and loading 220 tons before her engine room took up some of the hold. On a passage to Bristol she was caught off Land's End in a force 6 and rolled so badly that the steel sprit became bent and he had to go back into Penzance. The great difference between flat-bottomed barges and West Country vessels was that 'in a blow' the barges 'rolled their gear to windward' while the deep draft West Country vessels gripped the water and remained heeling, which reduced the strain aloft.

George bought Snape Maltings, a huge set of redundant Victorian industrial buildings standing alone at the top of the River Alde, in 1965. His first plan had been to reopen the wharf as a port, but local people claimed that, in the twenty-six years since the sailing barge *Beatrice Maud* had taken the last freight of barley, the channel had silted up. The five miles of river between Aldeburgh brickworks and Snape is a vast expanse of mud at low tide and finding the twisting channel at high tide can be difficult. The bargemen regarded Snape as being the most difficult place on the East Coast to reach.

The Gooderhams came with us on *Sea Fever* and we set out to sail up towards Snape. As we approached Slaughden Quay, the landing for Aldeburgh, I was amazed to see an elderly man in a heavy rowing boat who appeared to be determinedly trying to cross our bows. The wind was fresh and *Sea Fever* was lopping along well, but I had to come up into the wind to avoid the boat.

The man in the rowing boat was furious and shouted 'Little boats go to loo'ward!' As we swept past he handed me an invitation welcoming us to the Aldeburgh Yacht Club. This turned out to be Jumbo Ward, who acted as club boatman. I just saw a weather-beaten face and the sun caught on the gold ear-ring, which his generation of longshore men wore as protection against drowning. The voyage up to Snape then passed without incident and there proved to be plenty of water in the channel.

Motor barge traffic was restarted to Snape, then one Sunday night in the 'Plough and Sail', the subject came up about how on earth barges got up to the Maltings under sail. George looked thoughtful, he loved a new project, and said he would find a barge to make the trip.

On a warm night the following summer, George and I hurried along the river wall at Shotley, where a boat came ashore to take us to the sailing barge *Lord Roberts*. The barge was doing charter work and her owner Tony Winter rather liked the idea of being the first barge back to Snape. We left Harwich Harbour just after dawn on the last of the ebb tide and sailed along beside the low Suffolk coast. We reached Shingle Street, the little hamlet at the entrance to the river, at low water so that we had all the flood tide to get up some twenty miles to Snape.

The lower river was totally deserted, but when skipper Jim Lawrence spotted bird-watchers on Havergate Island it gave him an outlet for his own brand of dry Essex humour.

'Here', shouted Jim as the *Lord Roberts* swept past, 'is this the right river for Ipswich?' There was a surprisingly long pause before the reply came back 'you're in the wrong river!'

At Slaughden Quay Jumbo Ward came aboard to resume his old pre-war job of river pilot. Jumbo was a man living in the wrong century. He had grown up with his grandfa-

33. Aboard the barge *Lord Roberts* on the River Alde bound up to Snape. Jumbo Ward, Tony Winter and Jim Lawrence, 1966.

ther, who had piloted little schooners up to Snape in the Victorian period, and had retained the Suffolk speech and outlook of that far-away age. He had spent his whole life on the river between Iken and Slaughden and was well over seventy before a Russell Upson had taken him inland to the Midlands, where he had seen hills for the first time. Jumbo was amazed and thrilled and said he had no idea England was so big.

On the *Lord Roberts* Jumbo took up station on the lee deck, peering around the mainsail and giving advice such as 'luff up a bit old matee round that withy and bear away to loo'ard to the little withy afore the cliff'.

'There is a lump here soon' said Jumbo and almost at once the leeboards started to churn up grey mud. Two strong men worked like demons on the winch to get the leeboard off the bottom.

The barge kept moving, 'I'll wind her' shouted Jim spinning the wheel like mad. Round she came on to another tack. Hardly was she moving again when Jumbo ordered the foresail down and the 84ft barge to come up into the wind. The tide swept her up a short reach with mainsail and topsail 'frapping'. Up went the foresail again, pulling the head around into a new reach.

'Make a fetch to the next withy', commanded the veteran pilot, pointing to a branch sticking out of the water, 'keep her just to weather'.

This routine was enacted many times. Sometimes Snape Maltings was ahead over the bows and in some places as the channel wound around we could see it over the stern. Once USAF jet fighters, warriors of the unfought Cold War, screamed overhead, but we were simply not in the same century.

The sight of a barge turning to windward up the narrow channel alarmed the crews of a couple of local yachts anchored off Iken Cliff. We squeezed past the first yacht and then Jim locked the wheel, calmly walked to the side and, looking down at the worried face, remarked 'We'll get up old mates but watch out for the big steamer coming up astern'.

Jim Lawrence called this 'creek sailing', but with her flat bottom and little draft the *Lord Roberts* was in her element. She was built in 1900 as a Maldon 'stackie' barge with a low bow to reduce windage going up creeks to load stacks of straw and hay for the street horses of Victorian London. The *Lord Roberts* slowly wound her away up between the flooded marshes to the great brick buildings of Snape Maltings. For the last few reaches the only sail set was the lowered topsail sheeted out to the spreet end and this alone gave her steerage way.

It was hard work, but in skilful hands the barge did it. In the end we cheated and the engine was put on as we turned to go alongside the quay. A small crowd gathered and someone asked 'was it difficult to get that big boat up this tiny river?' 'No' we lied, 'she just came up on her own.'

The *Lord Roberts* had been 'cut down' to a motor barge for her final years in trade and Tony Winter had rigged her out again for holiday charters using the second-hand gear from over twenty barges. The mainmast was the one used by the *Queen* in the 1937 Coronation Barge Races, the sprit from the *Marie May*. In fact there was a story telling how every sail, spar and block had found its way on to this ageing wooden barge.

Having re-introduced barges to Snape, it seemed a good idea to get one up to the Pool of London again. With this in mind, we joined the *Lord Roberts,* this time with Tony Winter as skipper, in the autumn of 1967. The *Lord Roberts* was lying at the old brick-works quay at Lower Halstow, one of the many Back Creeks of the Kentish River Medway. Between us and the Medway was a vast area of saltings and marsh islands, while inland rose the Kent Downs.

We left Queenborough, famous then amongst barging people for its free berths and the awful smell of the glue works. On the last of the ebb, we left the Swale and came out past Sheerness into Sea Reach at the mouth of the Thames. The plan was that we would sail with the flood tide under us up the Thames to the buoys at Woolwich, but the wind was light and we had only reached Erith Rands by high water. Daylight was fading, but since there were no commercial wharfs or buoys we could lie on, the oil navigation lights were lit, and we crept on against the powerful ebb tide. We were going to anchor in Halfway Reach, but the prospect of being downwind of the Southern Outfall Sewerage Works made us go on slowly in the cool night air until the anchor was let go out of the way of commercial shipping under Leather Bottle Point. There was a mass of cranes and lights ahead in the Royal Docks and all around us was industrialisation, but when we came on deck there were mallard duck feeding on the water around us in the moonlight.

Next day, we took the flood up river again, but now it was blowing force 6-7. In Gallions Reach the barge, for all her beamy stackie hull, heeled and charged forward like an old war horse, leaving a white wake on the black water. Our skipper-owner gave worried glances aloft to see if any of his veteran gear would carry away, but it all held. Then quite suddenly in Bugsby Hole the wind left us and the barge spun round on the tide after rounding

Blackwall Point. The wind suddenly returned and the crew of a tug looked mildly surprised to see an old barge come charging around the point. Eventually we sailed quietly between the miles of empty nineteenth century brick warehouses and reached the totally deserted Lower Pool of London. Just below Tower Bridge the Thames River Police came alongside and said it was a long time since they had seen a barge under sail so far up the London River. The Thames was not a welcoming river, there was nowhere to berth and a fierce tide and the commercial shipping made anchoring risky.

In Victorian times the East Coast smacks used to sail up to Billingsgate Fish Market in the Pool of London with the first of the season's oysters. In 1972 the Worshipful Company of Fishmongers organised the Thames Oyster Race as a way promoting oyster sales. I joined the 46ft Whitstable smack *Rosa & Ada,* which Tony Winter had restored in Oare Creek, at Gravesend for the first oyster smack race up the Thames. Fifteen Essex and Kent smacks, each with a barrel of Whitstable oysters on board, came to the starting line off Gravesend at low water. This time the tide carried us through a ghost port above the Royal Docks. There were some seven miles of empty quays and silent warehouses. Dick Harman's *ADC* won the race, *Rosa & Ada* was fourth and all the smacks reached the finish at Cherry Garden Pier in about six hours.

Tower Bridge was lifted and, dwarfed by its size, we went up to lie on a pier in the Pool of London. The real mystery was that all around us were screaming teenage girls and this went on far into the night. About midnight this mystery was solved. Down the pier walked a flashly dressed young American, behind him his manager carrying money in bags and behind him a Cockney taxi driver carrying suitcases of clothes.

We asked the taxi-driver what this was all about. He, in true 'I have seen it all before' Cockney fashion replied drily 'It's David Cassidy going off to his yacht, he thinks he's a pop star.'

We left next morning under power, towing the *Stormy Petrel,* Dick Norris' Whitstable smack, which did not have an engine. When the wind picked up *Stormy* was cast off and the sails set. In the Lower Hope and Sea Reach, in strong winds and smooth waters, the *Rosa & Ada* was sailing at 9 knots. The smack was sailing like a terrier after a rat around the Isle of Sheppey and heading for her mooring in the Swale. Tony called for a reef in the main and then another. It was a great struggle for Roger and me to get the sail area reduced. The smacks, although they are half the size of a barge, are more difficult to handle because they have no winches and everything is a dead haul.

Long after the *Rosa & Ada* was sold, Tony Winter and his sons sailed the Wash smack *Unity* and then he bought the Bristol Channel pilot cutter *Mascotte.* I had first seen the *Mascotte* as a rotting hulk at Rye and then Paul Kennard saved this pilot cutter when he rebuilt her between 1980-87. Next, she was sold to a brewery in South Wales which was going to have her as a 'historical feature' berthed in front of a new dock-side pub. This proved a non-starter when the brewery discovered that the 60ft *Mascotte* drew 10ft while their pub's berth only had 5ft of water. One wonders if the consultant who had come up with this scheme got a Christmas bonus, anyway the *Mascotte* was back on the market at half the price.

Eventually the cutter was taken to Tommi Nielsen's yard at Gloucester Dock, was completely stripped out and converted back to the deck layout, rig and cabins of a pilot cutter of the Edwardian period. Another highly successful case of the past being recreated. We joined her in March 1998 as she left her winter berth at Nielsen's yard to go Around The Land to Plymouth. Our departure from Gloucester Dock just before Easter was silent and

34. Tony Winter's Bristol Channel pilot cutter *Mascotte* at Tommi Nielsen's yard, Gloucester Dock, 1998.

35. The Pilot cutter *Mascotte* waiting for the Sharpness Bridge to open. In the background on the left is the River Severn and to the right the Gloucester & Sharpness Canal, 1998.

well organised. The *Mascotte* passed the schooner *Kathleen & May* and other ships await-ing repair and purred off down the Gloucester and Sharpness Canal. The sixteen miles to Sharpness went without problems, but to lock out into the River Severn meant a lengthy delay while waiting for a bridge to be opened. In the late afternoon two workmen appeared and hand-cranked an ancient road bridge open and we moved down into Sharpness Dock and waited to lock out into the fierce tide of the River Severn.

The plan had been to stay at Sharpness overnight and then go down to Penarth the next day, but the radio was forecasting a Force 8 gale and snow on high ground. Tony decided to make a night passage to get down the Severn before the bad weather arrived. A 5000 tonne freighter had locked out ahead of us at 6.30pm. The tide had eased enough for the pilot to take her out into the last of the flood, but even then when she cleared the pier heads her bow was swept around by the tide and she stood still fighting the tide before heading off down towards the Bristol Channel.

At 7pm the sun came out from behind the clouds and we locked out into the Severn. The Estuary was wide, and apart from the one freighter ahead, totally empty. Across the river was the abandoned port of Lydney where, until fifty years before, the schooners and ketches had come to load coal. The tides run so strong in the Severn that the tugs only had a few minutes at slack water to tow the schooners into Lydney. Once the ebb with its 40ft fall started it was not safe to try and get the vessels into the tiny harbour mouth.

It was only as we approached the two Severn Road Bridges in the dusk that our speed on the ebb became apparent. To go under the first bridge meant crossing from the shore close to Beachley and going across the stream to reach the centre of the bridge. The

36. Pearl and Tony Winter on the *Mascotte*, largest of the Bristol Channel pilot cutters, leaving Sharpness, 1998.

Mascotte is a powerful craft, but the force of the tide swept her sideways. Once under this bridge we quickly shaped away for the next one and this time we had to keep exactly in the channel known as the Shoots. Here the tide funnels down between the English Stones, a rocky outcrop on the east shore, and more rocks on the Welsh side. In the Shoots the whirlpools swept branches, driftwood, and in one place a dead sheep around. High above, heavy lorries, just black boxes against the night sky, crossed from Somerset to Gwent while with the tide running at 10 knots and the *Mascotte* making 6 knots we were going over the ground at a water-skiing speed.

Below the Shoots both shores were lit up by Avonmouth and the towns of South Wales and it was very difficult to pick out the buoys in the darkness. Once off Portishead we tried to motor back to a buoy and read its name, but *Mascotte* could make no progress against the ebb and this was abandoned.

After Portishead the great yellow patch of light in the darkness on the Welsh shore marked the town of Newport. Here in 1904 a crusty old pilot called Thomas Cox and the shipwright William Stacy had built the 60ft *Mascotte*, the largest of the Bristol Channel pilot cutters. At that time the coal trade from South Wales was booming and there was a constant stream of ships inward and outward bound. The independent pilots were some of the top earners amongst the inshore maritime communities of the late Victorian and Edwardian period, but as ships grew larger the pilots amalgamated and bought steam cutters. The Newport pilots formed a group in 1914 and after this Thomas Cox used the *Mascotte* for racing, until he sold her for a yacht in 1919.

Cox was a hard man, once apparently riding all day on a Newport tram when they refused to put him off where he asked. He stayed on the tram until, on the last run of the day, they finally put him down at the spot he requested. The Coxes, all called Thomas, stayed with the Newport pilotage for another four generations and the last one retired in 1995. However they are overtaken by another family at Bristol who have been pilots there for seven generations.

In the moonlight the Isles of Steep Holme and Flat Holme showed up and next the *Mascotte* was crossing the mouth of the Severn towards the bright lights of Cardiff and Penarth. Now came heavy rain which in the English West Midlands caused the Easter Floods, the worst within living memory, resulting in loss of life and massive damage to property. By 11.30 we were in Penarth Roads, but had to wait four hours before there was enough water in the channel through construction work on the new Cardiff Bay Barrage to get into Penarth. To a well-founded ship in capable hands the fierce tides of the Severn and Bristol Channel are not a real problem, but these waters do not allow for mistakes. Once a port is left at high water there is nowhere a boat can enter until the next high tide.

The Winters, father and son, Tony and Paul, used the four dark and wet hours motoring around Penarth Roads as a 'board meeting' to work out the possibility of using the *Mascotte* for Management Training courses. Then at 4am in very heavy rain she finally entered the Marina at Penarth and berthed at the Town Quay. We left the pilot cutter with heavy rain driving against the cliffs of Penarth. Her planned trip on to Plymouth was postponed because a wild Force 8 was blowing in the Atlantic.

Chapter Six

DREDGING IN THE CHESAPEAKE

Before dawn on the eastern Atlantic seaboard of the United States, I peered into the darkness trying to count the number of skipjacks. There was no wind as we went out of Tilghman Island with the yawl or 'push-boat' shoving us along from astern. When the wind got up and the yawl was hauled up on the stern davits, the huge jib headed mainsail and great jib on a bowsprit were hoisted. As the first streak of daylight appeared on the horizon I began counting the white sails. There were nineteen skipjacks, all heading out into Chesapeake Bay for another day's oyster dredging. I had joined the 55ft skipjack *E C Collier* at Tilghman Island in the early hours of the morning. Her crew of seven had been just shapes in the dark, but as the day grew lighter I could see her Captain and owner John Larrimore standing at the wheel.

The year was 1976 and America had already landed a man on the moon, but here on her eastern seaboard there were still around forty boats registered for dredging or 'harvesting' oysters under sail only.

37. End of the day's dredging, a pusher yawl powers a skipjack back into Tilgham Island, Maryland, 1976.

This was in the Fall and I had already been up to Maine near the Canadian border looking at the 'dude' schooners which carried passengers on summer vacation. These lovely schooners, mostly owned by their own captains, were marketed and operated in a very efficient way, but they were not quite my idea of work boats with roots in the nineteenth century. We travelled south to the Chesapeake, a 195 mile long estuary cutting into the eastern seaboard, in search of the last working sail boats in north America.

The night before 'Peanut' Carter had won the Presidential election. 'He's my man' cried one of the black crew. Then someone asked me where I came from and there was a lack interest when I said 'England'.

Then came 'How you get here?' and I replied that I had come down from New York. This got a murmur of interest. Clearly the fact that I had come from the 'Big Apple' was much more important that any European destination. There were no further questions about New York and I was never certain whether any of the seven crew, of whom only two were white, had even been there. The eastern shore of the Chesapeake had never enjoyed the great wealth created by big industrial centres of the United States. It did not even have tourism and had remained a poor rural backwater, which was why the skipjacks had survived. That and the fact that about a century before someone had made a law banning power boats from dredging oysters. It had been intended to stop steam dredgers destroying the natural wild stock of oysters and had in fact kept alive this unique fleet of work boats.

Back on the wharf at Tilghman, Captain John and his cousin Captain Stanley Larrimore of the *Lady Kate* had had a very quiet discussion about where they were going to go dredging. The destination was referred to as 'up the river' and it was obvious that all the other skipjacks were heading in the same direction. In fact we all went for the Choptank River but all the skipjack captains had different ideas of the best place to find oysters. The Larrimores had obviously picked out a spot near the Choptank light.

A few trial dredges were made and then the captains exchanged waves to signal they had found a patch of oysters on the river bed and a marker buoy was thrown over. The rest of the working day was spent sailing in tight circles around it. Although the state law said the boats could not be power-driven, the huge dredges, one on each side, were hauled on deck by a motor. The captain gave the order, just a slight cough, and the dredges were pushed over the side and dragged along the bottom for a 'lick' of about three minutes. Then the captain pulled the cord to trip the motor 'winder' into gear and the dredges came back on to the deck where the contents fell out. The crew, three men each side, then sorted out the oysters by hand. It was cold, back-breaking work.

The captain stayed at the wheel all day, apart from when the wind increased and the crew had to reef the sails, he did all the sail handling. He manoeuvred the great wooden centreboarder with great skill around the buoy. The motor winder thundered away and the crew chucked the old shells overboard and the good oysters into piles, but Captain John was not satisfied and began to hassle his crew in a manner in which I presume the foremen of the old Southern cotton plantations had once used on their field workers.

'You god dam lazy ..... get your buts up in the air or we a'it never goner get our quota today.'

There was nothing in the least politically correct about the working language aboard this skipjack, but no one seemed offended, nor did they increase their pace. They had probably heard it all before. Only once did any comment come from the kneeling men, when Peewee said 'Oh Captain Johnny you is really bugging me...' Then Captain John drowned out any

38. Crew sorting the oysters on the deck of the skipjack *E C Collier* with skipjack *Lady Katie* ahead. 1976.

further comment by tripping the winch and up came another great heap of shells and rubbish to be sorted.

The boat's earnings were split three ways, first to the boat and her running costs and then divided amongst the seven men aboard. The oystermen aboard the skipjacks recognised that to earn more than the average manual worker in the area they had to fill the 150 bushel daily quota to achieve it, but it was hard work. As well as the great race against the time limit, it was also a matter of pride to see which boat would be the first to fill. In the mid-afternoon someone pointed across the Choptank to two triangular-sailed skipjacks which were heading back towards Tilghman.

'That's the *H W Krentz* leading', said Captain John dryly. He was not going to give any compliments and then he added 'two more licks and we will have got our quota same as him'.

The truth was the deck was piled high with oysters and everyone was pleased. A good earning day in November helped to offset any loss of time later in the winter when there was ice on the Chesapeake or they could not go out in the gales.

When the long clipper bow of the *E C Collier* was heading towards Tilghman, where the trucks were ready to haul the oysters off to restaurants all over the Unites States, Captain John became more chatty. He told me he was sixty-seven years old and had no intention of retiring.

39. Captain Johnny Larrimore at the wheel of the skipjack *E C Collier*. 1976.

'Drudging is the best god dam job on the water', he said, giving the wheel a tug, 'just so long as I can crawl aboard and have the strength to stand at the wheel I am going oystering'. His crew did not share this enthusiasm and just talked about the likely dollar value of the day's work.

And what of the future of skipjacks working under sail? Captain John shrugged his shoulders, and like everyone else around the Chesapeake said, 'they a'it going to last much longer'. The tongers, motor boats, which picked the oysters up with long tongs, were much cheaper to operate.

Over the next decade and a half, the number of skipjacks slowly declined. Many were eagerly bought by museums, and this was the fate of the *E C Collier*. About a decade later she was hauled ashore at the Chesapeake Bay Maritime Museum at St Michael's and became the centre of an oystering exhibit. Then the law over using yawls to power-dredge was relaxed so that the skipjacks could do two days in the working week powered by their yawls. This meant that the skipjacks only went out on the two 'push days' and they were only getting 50-70 bushels. In 1998 there were still ten boats doing this and the *Kathryn* and *Rebecca T Ruark* were going out on occasional sail days, but only to show their fare-paying passengers what dredging under sail was like.

Fishermen are the world's worst conservationists. They never leave anything for to-morrow. The whole idea of the Maryland ruling of 'no power boat' oyster-dredging had

40. Chesapeake Bay skipjack *H W Krentz* in the Choptank River, 1976.

been to strike the balance between allowing the men to earn a living, but put in a handicap so that they did not exhaust the oyster stocks in one gloriously profitable bonanza. It had worked well on the Chesapeake and it was equally effective in preserving the oyster stocks and the world's last fleet of sailing dredgers near Falmouth in the west of England.

In the spring of 1969 I met Mike Parsons fitting out his 24ft sail boat *Lelia*, which he had built himself, at the head of Mylor Creek. Mike said that if I returned the following autumn I was welcome to come dredging with him. The principle of gathering wild oysters from the bed of Carrick Roads was exactly the same as in the Chesapeake, but the Cornishmen used small hand-haul dredgers worked from half-decked gaff cutters. They sailed out the short distance from Flushing, Mylor, Restronguet and Pill to work on the 'banks' of wild oysters they found along the channel of Carrick Roads.

On either side of this mile wide stretch of sheltered water the green hills of Cornwall rose to the distant highland. There were nineteen 'sail boats' dredging in Carrick Roads that year and I was surprised to find there was no written history of these boats and even more surprised to find out that the price of oysters justified building new boats. Mike said all my questions about the work boats' past and future could be answered by the boat-builder Terry Heard, but it was not until 1974 that I plucked up courage to go and see the mentor of the Cornish dredgermen.

Terry Heard was a tall, bearded man who greeted me like a friend and was delighted that someone was trying to work out the history of 'our boats'. He had bought a cottage beside Mylor Creek and created the Tregatreath boatyard which was filled with yachts and Truro River workboats. Sitting in the cottage on a cold December Sunday afternoon he told me he had started as a dredgerman, but in 1961 he had built his first workboat, the 29ft *Result*, a rather narrow boat because she had been built in a garage.

In 1963 a very severe winter wiped out virtually all the oyster stocks on the East Coast of England and this pushed up the price of Cornish oysters. The Cornishmen had expected their sail boats to fade away after World War II, but suddenly in the 1960s the business became highly lucrative and they started to think about replacing their very mixed bunch of work boats, most dating from before 1914. It was a unique situation because most work boat types were facing extinction, while Terry Heard was about to create a new generation of boats referred to as the Falmouth Work Boats.

Terry built four wooden work boats and did up many more, but the time involved with a wooden hull made them too expensive and working men turned to fibreglass hulls. This has created a new generation of work boats, some still used for dredging in the winter. The fishery has always fluctuated and in the 1980s an oyster disease almost wiped it out, but stocks recovered and some days in the winter of 1997-98 there were twenty-two sail boats dredging. The Heards, Terry and now his son Martin, have also developed a new type of work boat, with large and more expensive sail plans, which are just raced in the summer.

Chapter Seven

BAREFOOT DOWN THE CARIBBEAN ISLANDS

The day I left *Fantome* in 1972 to fly home, Captain Terry Bewley said to me 'it must have been quite a shock for you coming out like that straight from London'. It was my first long-haul flight and when I stepped out on to the runway in Antigua the heat of the night was almost overpowering. I hired a cheerful taxi driver to take me to the ship and although he chatted away for the whole trip, I could understand very little of his West Indian English. It was a great relief to arrive at the quay in the Deep Water Harbour where I could just make out the four-masted schooner *Fantome* in the dark.

Aboard, Captain Terry Bewley and Danish stewardess Katie were welcoming passengers, but all I wanted to do was sleep. Totally unaware that the air-conditioning system had broken down, I lay in my cabin sweltering and unable to sleep. The American passengers in the next cabin were in the same state of exhaustion and celebrated the fact by having a swearing match that went on all night with the occasional bang when one of them threw something.

By the time dawn came I had begun to wish I had not come on this trip. Then, going on deck, I saw the green of the hills around the St John's Deep Water Harbour and suddenly felt this was the most beautiful place in the world. Actually St John's is pretty average by West Indian standards, but this was a totally new world to me. I was amazed to find that most people, when faced with the sweltering heat, had simply come up and slept on deck under the stars. Later in the afternoon we sailed and then I was really impressed, the sea was deep blue and the warm breeze meant one could stand on deck in shorts.

The 220ft *Fantome* was a steel four-masted schooner built in 1927 as a private yacht for the Duke of Westminster. The Duke had started to convert a wooden American cargo schooner to a yacht, but found the hull too far-gone so he had switched to having a steel version built as the *Flying Cloud*. The Guinness family renamed her *Fantome* and she was berthed in Seattle when World War II started and stayed there until she was bought by Captain Mike Burke for his Windjammer Cruises.

In 1947 Mike Burke had started his cruise ships by running trips in his yacht *Hangover*. During the day Mike and his friends sailed and in the evening they partied in the local bar. Keeping to this relaxed formula Mike started to buy bigger boats for his cruises and then realised that there were still large sailing yachts laid up all over the world which their owners could not sell. Mike Burke's Windjammer Cruises bought big ships cheaply and fitted them out for passenger-carrying. The *Fantome* had spent several years at Miami having her millionaire's accommodation replaced by cabins for American passengers.

Each Windjammer schooner was based at a West Indies island which had good air links with the States. Once the passengers were aboard there was no fixed schedule, the Captain sailed to whichever island he wished. Most sailing was done at night so the passengers could spend the days exploring, swimming or snorkelling. Although always in contact with the head office in Miami, Captain Terry ran the ship from his tiny cabin just aft of the forward bridge. He was an Englishman trained on the Union Castle Line and most of his afterguard were Europeans, with some Americans. On many islands the sight of the captain coming ashore resulted in West Indians running along the beach in the hope of getting a deck job on the big schooner.

The passengers were encouraged to help with sail-handling and steering if they liked, and most did, but this was purely voluntary. Many did serious sun-bathing, and nearly all turned out to party at night. The Windjammer fleet were staysail schooners and so engines did most of the work. Sail-handling was not a major problem, when the giant four-master tacked the only sail handled was a staysail which had to be lifted over the head of the person at the wheel.

'Watch her, she's wicked', said Eddie in his rolling West Indian English as he stood on the bridge beside me at the wheel, 'she wiggles like a woman, like a woman who say, oh don't touch me there!'

It was a fair description of *Fantome's* sailing. Once when sailing at night she decided to sail straight for the Redonda rock. The low economy of the Caribbean provided few navigational aids and the islands were mostly recognised by the lights of the houses ashore. The Redonda showed up as a black mass against a moonlit sky and *Fantome* could only be lured away from it by easing off the spanker sail so that her bow did not keep turning up into the wind.

In the night we passed Guadeloupe, officially part of France and now part of the European Union. The British or Beewee islands had nearly all been given independence, but France had come up with the clever idea of claiming her former colonies were

41. Windjammer's 4-masted schooner *Fantome* off Nevis, Leeward Islands, 1972.

actually part of 'Belle France' so that the islands stayed in their control. In the morning we were off the French Iles des Saintes and it was like something out of a Joseph Conrad story. We went up a narrow channel with the cliffs rising high above us on either side and then we came out into a sheltered bay in front of a tiny town. The anchor roared down and the launch was soon ferrying us ashore.

These islands had first been settled by the Breton fishermen, so the islanders still had fair skins and the women were taller than those on most West Indian islands. When the tropical evening started the *Fantome's* generator broke down and the ship was plunged into total darkness. Dull thumps came from the engine room as the engineers worked to restore the light. There were no showers or ice in the beer, which the American passengers found very hard to take. They started plotting. Say, let's go over to the jetty, hire the big ferry boat, say ten bucks a head, and go over to a hotel in Guadeloupe. Captain Terry, veteran of many Windjammer problems, said cheerfully 'right now no one needs an iced beer or water' and refused to put the launch back in the water.

Spontaneously two New York opera singers, with the help of taped music, gave us a full-blooded Italian performance on the poop. It was magical. At midnight the generator roared back into life and amid wild excitement the *Fantome* put to sea and sailed north of Montserrat. Here, under the shadow of the British flag at the Governor's House, I ran into a little local difficulty. In the Leeward Islands the sugar industry had largely died and, apart from overseas aid, tourism was the only way money came into the islands. Most of the hotels were owned by New York money and my new American friends claimed to be able to tell which hotels were owned by Mafia money, and they generated a few kick-backs to the local politicians. The average West Indian still lived in a shack, with little or no income. To try and take money from tourists they charged a dollar for every photograph which included them or their house. I was totally unaware of this custom and on taking a street scene in Montserrat found a large number people suddenly demanding money because they claimed their houses, bicycles or whatever were in the view. I abandoned photography and headed for the nearest empty beach for a swim.

Generally speaking, the smaller islands were poorer and more relaxed and the people did not hassle for money. The *Fantome,* which drew 19ft of water, sailed on and anchored off St Eustatius. This Dutch island is only around two miles long and rises to a volcano peak in the centre. We anchored off the remains of one of the largest eighteenth century ports in North America, a centre of the sugar trade. The fort at Eustatius made the mistake of being the first place to salute the new United States flag during the American Revolution. Big mistake, Admiral Rodney turned up with the British fleet and bombarded the place flat. Later, during a volcanic eruption, most of the town slipped into the sea.

We had been sailing in the Caribbean for a week without seeing another ship, but on passage to Saba we spotted a tanker on the horizon. Saba is basically a huge rock rising 3000 ft out of the blue sea and in the eighteenth century, when the British, French and Dutch fought and squabbled over the islands, no-one bothered with Saba because there was no land to grow sugar. It became a pirate's hideaway and as there was no landing place they defended it by rolling rocks down on any unwelcome visitors. The Dutch government supported Saba's only industry, making up the two miles of road from the landing place to the village on the peak. Here the men, who went away in the Dutch merchant navy, had the Lion Club, modelled on a Rotterdam seamen's bar.

We sailed on, calling at St Maartens, where there was a cruise liner anchored in the bay, to the beautiful little island of St Barts and then north to the flat island of Anguilla. The

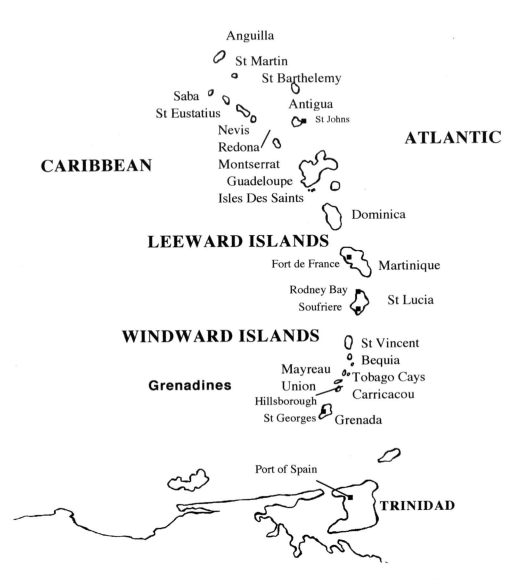

British Government, wanting to pull out of the expense of keeping up colonies, had put islands together in little groups and given them independence. However the islands all spoke different dialects of English and French and they hate and mistrust each other. Anguilla had kicked out its partner and demanded to become a British colony again and in a stroke of good judgement London policemen had been sent to sort out this minor revolution.

We anchored off Sandy Ground village where there was a fabulous and completely empty sandy beach. Because it is low-lying, Anguilla did not have tourism and was still trying to build and operate the little inter-island schooners. Lying out in the bay, flying a huge Union Jack, was a new schooner they had taken four years to build, while another one was hauled up on the beach for repair.

42. Windjammer's 3-masted schooner *Mandalay*. (*Paul Maskell*)

I thought at that time I had come too late to see working sailing vessels, but twenty-one years later I returned to the West Indies and found there were still sailing craft in the Grenadines, to the south. At first glance Antigua looked more prosperous this time, there was a new airport building and many houses, but people still lived in the same tiny wooden shacks on the harbour end of St John's. This time I joined Windjammer Barefoot Cruises' three-masted staysail schooner *Mandalay,* which had been built as a yacht in 1922. A tremendous farewell party was going on for passengers leaving the last trip. Also, supplies were being taken aboard from the Windjammer supply ship *Amazing Grace,* which had come down from Miami. We were due to sail some five hundred miles south to Grenada, but as there had been a great storm, Captain Tony Clynick headed north to Nevis, where he knew he would find shelter at Charlestown.

The weather was unsettled with heavy rain, at times very hard. A huge sea slopped aboard the *Mandalay* as we sailed north. At first glance Charlestown did not look to have changed at all. There was a new jetty and we walked out of the town hoping to find the beach where the *Fantome* party had barbecued, but palm trees had grown up and much of the area was fenced off and had become the sea front for large luxury houses. Windjammer had changed too, it had become a much more professional outfit, no breakdown this trip. The competition had become very much keener. Now there were many cruise ships in the Caribbean and quite a lot of these were sailing vessels.

We saw several sailing cruise ships, including the huge schooner *Club Mediterranean, Windstar* and one moonlit night we passed close to the four-masted barque *Sea Cloud* with most of her thirty-two sails set. Windjammer crews and their loyal passengers very much resented rival sailing cruisers coming into what for decades had been just their territory, but they loathed the huge cruise liners which were then arriving in ever larger numbers. When we were heading for the tiny Grenadines island of Mayreau the vast white P & 0 cruise liner *Sea Princess* passed us, towering over the tiny *Mandalay* like a block of flats.

'I know what to do !' roared the Irish mate Mike Taylor as he rushed off to get a small cannon. Although only firing blanks, this was now aimed at the *Sea Princess* and he started to bang away while our American and few European passengers shouted abuse at the liner. On the poop other passengers, male and female, lined up and mooned the liner. The message was in vain, the *Sea Princess,* a great white palace towering above us, gave a reluctant toot and continued on her way to collect her passengers ashore on the P & 0 private Mayreau beach.

Mayreau had been abandoned and the people had moved across to St Vincent in search of work, but after P & O started calling here once a fortnight, people moved back and opened up bars and shops. However, the arrival of about a thousand people on any lonely beach does rather alter the place. Once I thought we had reached a true tropical island when we came into the empty lagoon at Tobago Cays. The people from nearby Union Island had seen the *Mandalay* making for the island and came across in speed boats and hung up tee shirts between the palm trees to sell. In search of peace we walked across the tiny island and found another lagoon, this time with over forty yachts anchored there. It is hard to find a deserted paradise in the Lesser Antilles.

On St Lucia we anchored in Rodney Bay, which had been the headquarters of the British men-of-war. All the islands to the north down the trade winds are Leeward Islands, while those to the south are Windward Islands. At the head of Rodney Bay there was a vast new yacht marina and hotel complex which had given much-needed work to the island. At the other end of St Lucia we had appeared to be sailing straight into the side of a mountain, but in a slight bay we were just able to make out the houses of Soufriere under palm trees.

The brightly-painted fishing canoes with their huge Japanese outboards were hauled up on the beach and this relaxed and beautiful place seemed like paradise. A young man attached himself to us and said he was our guide. He took as on a conducted tour around the streets of the village, mostly single-storey corrugated tin houses. The women and children, all smartly dressed in bright clothes, were just coming out of the Roman Catholic Church. It seemed the local church custom was for the women to go one day and the men had their own service the next day and after that 'everybody party'. We went for a beer and our guide told us that his one aim in life was to leave and go and join his aunt in Brixton. I was surprised and asked why he wanted to leave this beautiful place, Soufriere and the Pitons peaks appear in most luxury holiday brochures. He explained that he was twenty-eight-years old and had never had a regular job. Last month he had only earned £28 from tourists. To him Soufriere seemed like prison and he did not see it as one of the world's most attractive places.

One breezy night, when passing on the Caribbean side of Montserrat, the *Mandalay* with lower staysail and headsail set got up to eight knots. As the gaff schooner *Hussar* she had had a reputation for speed and was credited with sailing at fourteen knots. On the open deck the quiet American mate Matt Thomas was very pleased with her progress. The schooner had not been in the company's dry dock in Trinidad for two years, so under water

43. The *Mandalay* leaving Surfriere, St Lucia in the Windward Islands with the Pitons ahead, 1993.

the hull must have been pretty foul. The *Mandalay* ploughed on, throwing up spray while the rain beat down on her empty decks. In the light from the binnacle we could just see the faces of Matt and seaman Selwyn. Matt was constantly checking our position with the lights on the mountain side of Montserrat but Selwyn took no interest in this island. However it was very different a few nights later when we saw the lights of St Vincent. 'That's my island', he announced proudly and claimed he could see the lights of his home. The *Mandalay* passed St Vincent every fortnight, but Selwyn had not been home for over a year.

As we approached the high cliffs and green peaks of Grenada, Matt was busy with the crew and some passengers hoisting all the sails and said to me 'you take the wheel, you are one of the few who comes on here who enjoys the sailing'.

Captain Tony had all the sails set so that the schooner looked her best and we could go off and take photographs of her. They were still coiling down the halliard and had just lowered the launch when a fierce squall came from nowhere. The great schooner heeled over like a racing yacht and surged off with the wind screaming through her rigging. At the same time, a tremendous downpour of rain soaked the mates and deck crew as they rushed around letting go every halliard to get most of the sails down. As quickly as it had begun, the squall was gone and we came out of the rain to find two cruise liners anchored off St George's, on the southern end of Grenada. Mike Taylor was off at once to get his cannon and the passengers shouted 'ramming speed Captain!'

69

44. Matt Thomas about to sail the *Mandalay's* small spritsail Bequia whaler, 1993.

The huge cruise liners had to stay anchored at sea, but the smaller Windjammer ships could get up into the harbour at St George's. The attractive harbour is a very sheltered inlet with land rising steeply on three sides. The houses cling to the hills, although down on the quay some of the nineteenth century administration buildings were in ruins after being burnt down when Cuba had sent in troops to impose a Communities Government and Americans sent in troops to restore the elected Government.

The Grenada Invasion had been several years before, but there were bullet scars in the houses and there was a faded sign painted on a building saying 'Welcome Americans. Thank You'. The American passengers from *Mandalay* were astounded to read this.

The inter-island traders and fishing boats call to unload at the head of St George's Harbour. From here the wooden 'schooners', *Beatrice* and the *Edna David*, took on passengers and small parcels of freight north to the smaller islands in the Grenadines. Although called schooners they were actually big motor sloops, but once clear of St George's up went the sails so that the trade winds could aid their three and half hours trip to Hillsborough on Carriacou. When we were there in 1993 they were fitting out a motor ship for this Hillsborough ferry run, so it was relief to return two years later and see the local people lowering their belongings on to the deck of the *Beatrice*, this stronghold of sail had survived.

The first person we met was Mike Taylor, very proud of having become master of the *Mandalay*, but we were joining the other Windjammer schooner moored across the harbour. This was the 176ft three-masted schooner *Yankee Clipper*, typical of cruise schooners operated by the Burke family in the Caribbean. Built as the yacht *Cressida* in

70

45. The 3-masted schooner *Mandalay* in St George's Harbour, Grenada, 1993.

1927, the *Yankee Clipper* had been going continually up and down the islands for over thirty years. Her master, when we joined, was the bristling Scotsman Neil Carmichael, who spent a lot of time worrying about how he was going to get his golf handicap down.

When we reached Carriacou we took a Hillsborough bus, actually one of the many vans on hire, across the tiny airport runway to Tyrrel Bay. Here Gordon Compton was still building a big wooden 'schooner'. In two years there had not been much progress because payment from the future owner was slow. Gordon thought this would be the last wooden inter-island trader he would build, but there was plenty of work repairing the wooden 'schooners'.

One afternoon the *Yankee Clipper* anchored off Morpion, a sandbank to the north of Carriacou, to let us swim and snorkel. In the late afternoon we saw four fishing boats, smart sloops with jib-headed mainsails, beating back towards the small island of Petit Martinique. In Port Elizabeth on Bequia the inter-island schooner *Friendship Rose* lay on her anchor at the head of the inlet. She had been last of the two-masted inter-island schooners under sail in the Windward and Leeward Islands. Built on the island in 1969, she had been on the ferry run across to St Vincent and even after a motor ship took over, many people stayed loyal to the schooner. Finally, in 1992, she was forced to give up and after this she was converted for charter trips. The only other two-masted Caribbean schooner we saw was the Carriacou-built *Scaramoo* which was running day tourist trips from Union Island. The freight imported through Trinidad came up to other islands in battered old European coasters. We even saw a Thames flat iron collier lying in Port of Spain.

71

46. Building a new schooner at Gordon Compton's Tyrrel Bay, Carriacou in 1993. The Grenadines remained one of the pockets of wooden boat building and working sail-using vessels.

47. Athneil Ollivierre, king of the Bequia whalers, with a harpooner at his museum, 1995.

Many of the American passengers were deeply shocked to learn that Bequia was famous for its whaling and the islanders claimed this was still going on. During the season emigrating whales pass close to the Altantic side of Bequia and hand harpooners in small open sailing-rowing whalers would go out after them. In the afternoon we joined a party going over to Friendship Bay. Just off-shore was the tiny island to which the whales had been towed for boiling down. The only whale boat in Friendship Bay was the 27ft *Why Not*, which did not look as if she had been to sea for some time. They had not taken a whale since 1993 because the young men of Bequia preferred to pursue the Yankee dollar by making models of whaler boats rather than undertake a dangerous trip to kill those passing their island.

The last of the Bequia hand-harpooners was 74 year old Athneil Ollivierre, who with his tiny naive whaling 'museum', had become one of the island's main tourist attractions. Athneil spoke the rolling West Indian English, but as his name suggests, was a descendant of the Portuguese whalers who had settled on this side of the island about three hundred years before. All along the Caribbean islands there had been little pockets of white settlers who had kept themselves apart for centuries. On Dominica, on the wettest part of this island of heavy rainfall, there is a community of native North Americans. Shy, gentle and desperately poor people, they were looked down on by the dominant Afro-Caribbean population.

It was very clear weather on that trip and we could see the islands stretching away in a line in either direction, a series of mountain peaks rising out of clear blue sea. Matthew Bolton, Australian mate of the *Yankee Clipper,* told me that while sailing off St Lucia, he had once seen, from the deck, Guadeloupe nearly 200 miles away. While on Bequia, I noticed thick black smoke rising from the larger neighbouring island of St Vincent and thought it must be a forest fire. A local laughed and said 'no that is the volcano, no problem, it's been like that for several years'.

At that time Montserrat started to erupt and the situation became so bad that in 1997 the whole island was evacuated. The Caribbean, with its warm climate and beautiful islands, were the most perfect waters I had ever sailed in, but nowhere is without some drawbacks.

Union Island 1995

Dubai Creek 1997.

Chapter Eight

THE DHOW HARBOURS

The 1970 East Coast Old Gaffers' Race was an incredible event. It blew a gale and out of the eighty entrants, only fourteen started and of these just six got around the course. The first home was the Norfolk yoll *Amity* and *Fanny* won on corrected time. On *L'Atalanta,* we met a vicious short sea off the Colne Bar, blew out two jibs and retired rather ungracefully to Brightlingsea. Nine year-old Caroline was aboard and for safety we put her down below in the cabin. Later we found the coal-burning cabin stove had broken loose and she was down there dodging it as it crashed around the saloon.

The boat that really caught my eye in that race was the 39ft *Mjojo*, a gaff-rigged dhow which Rod Pickering and his family had just sailed back from East Africa via the Cape of Good Hope. Later that winter Rod showed us a film of her being built on the beach at Lamu and the Moslem shipwrights killing a goat to celebrate her launching. Not long afterwards, Ron set out to sail the Atlantic in a catamaran, but never reached the other side.

At Christmas 1986 Nick White said 'you really should go to Lamu, they build the dhows which go to India there'. I thought of the Pickering's flickering film show and the oiled hull of the *Mjojo* taking shape under the palm trees. In February we were snowed in, the lane down to our cottage was blocked. Sitting by the fire I thought of Lamu and suggested to Pearl that this would be a good time to go there. Pearl, who always sees the practical side of life, immediately started thinking of injections against tropical diseases.

Not many days later we were sitting on the edge of an East African air strip waiting to get the ferry across the wide fast-flowing estuary to Lamu. The women on the ferry boat all wore the Moslem black, but there were none of the inhibitions of the Arab world. As the boat crossed they sang, laughed and made the curious whaling sound beloved by African women. Lamu Island had a population of ten thousand, and only one car. The walled town, which had once been an Arab trading centre, had narrow alleys with sewage running down the gutters. It was all very relaxed and I loved the place at once.

Later a guide, David, showed us around the town and I asked about the dhow building. 'This is where they used to build the dhows', he said when we reached an empty beach just up river of the town. The palm trees were there, but the place was covered in rubbish from the town.

The large Lamu dhows which had once made an annual monsoon voyage to India with sugar were all gone. Sitting on the hotel balcony we saw about a dozen dhows going down river under sail loaded with mangrove poles for the building trade. They were about 40ft long with masts raked well forward. Outside on the waterfront a man greeted me with the instant friendliness of a Third World 'fixer' and asked if there was anything he could arrange for us. My request to see dhow building was quickly greeted with a promise to arrange this for £28. At the appointed time we were guided down to the beach were I found we had hired a small dhow with its crew of three men. I would have waded out, however the two Africans were determined to carry us sitting between them on their hands. I felt like Livingstone setting out to find the source of the Nile.

The captain smiled, but did not speak any English. He had elephantisis in one leg and chain-smoked, but seemed very happy sailing the dhow. Mohammed Famua acted as

48. Leaving the dhow village of Matendoni in the *Wasitara* as we run back down to Lamu, 1987.

guide and spoke good English, while the boy was very keen to learn about England. He asked what London was like and seemed impressed by my description of the crammed underground in the rush hour.

The open dhow *Wasitara* was about 25ft long, her woodwork finish was very rough, but the fine-lined hull was fast and very handy. When they tacked the dhow, the long yard of the lateen sail was pulled straight upright on the small mast and the sail was passed round to the other side. We quickly beat up river between the low mangrove swamps.

No-one said where we were going, but after a while we rounded a bend and there were the thatched rooves of Matendoni. Some of the village's thirty trading dhows were lying on a jetty and others under repair were hauled up under the shade of a palm leaf shelter. Although tourism was making an impact on the area, Matendoni was still a complete community revolving around sailing dhows.

'Follow me', said Mohammed Famua with a smile, 'I will show you how we live, but you are not allowed to take photographs of the dhows being built, it is forbidden'. The Kenyan Government believed it was demeaning for working people to be photographed. Having come so far, I found this hard to accept. I held the camera at waist level and clicked away. Back in Mombasa it was the same, only here there were armed police waiting to arrest any tourist unwise enough to photograph the motor dhows being discharged in the Old Harbour.

The dhows lay on the foreshore and streams of very strong porters walked up one gang-plank, took a sack on their backs and walked down another plank and then up to a warehouse. This is how the medieval ports of Europe must have looked.

Just above the Old Harbour was an empty beach which had been used by the big sailing dhows when they had come down on the monsoon voyages from the Arabian Gulf. We went to look at this area, but the midday heat under the cliffs was intense and while walking back into Mombasa I collapsed into a doorway. Both Pearl and I had suffered a major stomach-upset after visiting Lamu, but this time I had dehydrated in the heat. Luckily we were with John Jewell, a dhow expert and a doctor. Fortunately the doorway was at the house of an English friend of Jewell's and we were shown into a cool courtyard. Here I recovered quickly after a servant produced a glass of water.

There were many small dhows running trips off the glorious sandy beaches each side of Mombasa and I thought we had covered the subject until we met Flora Kirkland. She was half-owner of the dhow *Nawalilkher* (*Gateway to Heaven*) which was running tourist trips around Mombasa Harbour. This dhow, even with a shortened mast and an engine fitted, was a superb vessel. She was reputed to have been the last one built at Lamu for the Indian voyages. She had carried 110 tons, with a crew of seventeen to hoist the huge lateen sail. Her old trading captain was still with her, an aristocrat of the sea, who gave quiet orders in a tone that he knew would be obeyed.

Many of the dhows at the Old Harbour flew the flags of the Arab states, but it was not until 1997 that we travelled to the great trading centre of Dubai Creek in the United Arab Emirates. On the Gulf coast Dubai had constucted one of the world's largest man-made harbours where state-of-the-art container ships arrived from all over the western world. Many of the goods were then exported from Dubai Creek in the traditional dhows.

49. A fibreglass fishing dhow being hauled out of a scrub at the Al Boom Marine, Ajman, United Arab Emirates, 1997.

There were about two hundred traditional Gulf craft lying along the east bank of Dubai Creek. Some of these were fibreglass fishing dhows built in the nearby Sheikhdom of Ajman, but most were wooden craft. On the quay were piles of goods, with Arab merchants in their long white gowns hovering around while the loading was done by hand through small hatches by large crews of Indians. The friendly master of one 100 ton Dubai 'launch' noticed me taking photographs and offered to hire me his craft. I declined, but asked where he traded.

'Cigarettes and other goods to Yemen and Somalia' was the reply. He had a crew of seven and two 110hp Japanese diesels. 'Sometimes' said the Arab ship master with a huge smile, 'I need to go very fast'.

There is no such thing as smuggling in Dubai Creek. There is no tax or duty here and they can load and sell anything they like. Gold was very cheap in the nearby souk, the traders had a free hand to do what they liked so long as they did not offend the ruling family of Dubai or break the rules of the Moslem Koran.

I was told it took weeks to load these complicated cargoes. Engines, cars, cement, televisions, fruit, machinery, fish and everything else all went aboard with a lot of shouting. Some dhows went on month-long voyages around the Gulf, dropping part cargoes in tiny ports. It must have been an awful job remembering where everything was in the hold. The 100 ton launches were running across to Iran, while some 400-700 tonners were loading for Bombay, and they set a small lateen sail for the seven day voyage in the trade winds.

50. The largest wooden craft built in the Arabian Gulf under construction at the Al Khattal shipyard Dubai Creek, 1997. These were being built by one Saaed Al Khattal for one of his brothers.

Andrew Wilkins, a Brit expat working in the UAE, said Dubai Creek looked like Bristol docks in 1795. Indeed, Long John Silver would have been quite at home on this quay. Here was a form of trading which has totally vanished in the western world, yet in the Gulf it worked perfectly. More than that, business was booming. There was a steady stream of wooden dhows, with their bridges decorated with brightly-painted carvings, motoring in and out of the Creek under the shadow of the huge modern high-rise buildings.

Cutting across the Creek were two large modern road bridges and above these was the shipyard where the dhows were built. In the small, very neat office of Saaed Al Khattal's Al Garhound shipyard I was made welcome in perfect English, the working language of the Gulf. Take photographs, of course, and they were happy to answer any questions.

Outside were two of the largest wooden hulls I had ever seen under construction. The smell of freshly sawn hardwood was wonderful. Somewhere in the forest of Indonesia there must have been a very large gap to supply all the timber for these vessels, yet the craftsmanship was impressive. The motor dhows were being built by Indian shipwrights without plans in the traditional manner. The largest of these two craft was 1200 tons and took seventeen shipwrights twenty months to construct. By far the largest wooden dhow ever built.

Dubai Shipwright, 1997.

The Drift Net

K.C. Lockwood.

Trawling

K.C. Lockwood.

Chapter Nine

THE BEACH BOAT SAGA

Most of the East Coast of England has, over the centuries, had trouble with erosion. Perhaps the most dramatic loss has been on the Suffolk coast where the soft sandy land has slipped into the sea, taking with it the medieval town of Dunwich and its natural harbour, once the best in East Anglia. From Dunwich and other smaller ports, ships had sailed to the lucrative Icelandic cod fishery, but erosion dealt the coast a terrible blow and the homeless people were left in despair through lack of work. The remaining fishermen switched to working boats off the open beaches. This prospered on a modest scale and in the Victorian period there were around three hundred open boats working off the various beach landings, along the Suffolk coast.

A century later fish stocks had depleted and only a handful of fishermen worked off this coast. Most coastal villages, such as Thorpeness just north of Aldeburgh, had been developed for tourism and only a few part-time inshore fishing boats were kept on the beach. One dark December's night in 1975 I set off to Thorpeness to meet two elderly fishermen to learn something about their days working sailing boats off the beaches.

Back from the beach in a little red brick cottage I met Harry Harling, a ninety-one year old fisherman. He lived in the cottage where he was born and his grandfather had lived before he died in 1895. Harry also recalled that before 1914 fourteen full-time fishermen had worked off the beach. He had worked three types of Suffolk longshore boats, open clinker craft sometimes called punts because their bottoms were almost flat. These were all dipping luggers and were used for different types of fishing. The powerful 21-footer *Gypsy Queen* had been used for summer trawling, the 18ft *Industry* for herring and sprat

51. The day we bought the *Pet* on Thorpeness beach, 1981. Richard Wilson leaning on the *Shady Nook* while on the right Jonathan is walking towards the *Pet*.

drifting in the autumn because she was light enough to be rowed. The smaller 15ft boat was used for working lobster hoops on The Rocks, a patch of seabed just off-shore.

They had worked mostly within about three miles of the sheltered spot where they landed under the headland of Thorpe Ness. The boats were sailed whichever way the tide was going and they came back on the next tide. The big adventure of Harry's fishing career had been the time he and his mate Percy Westrup had gone trawling in *Gypsy Queen* some seven miles around Orfordness and down to Hollesley Bay. In the evening the wind dropped and they set out to row home. Arriving back late at night they found their families waiting on the beach with lanterns.

In a nearby cottage I met Percy Westrup who turned out to be the local folk singer, but he was not all that interested in talking about fishing under sail. I left Thorpeness and forgot about open luggers until Boxing Day, 1980 when we were at Orford and my fourteen year old son Jonathan came running around the corner saying he had found an open clinker hulk. We had been trying to find a genuine winkle brig to restore, but the hulk he had found turned out to be the 18ft Suffolk longshore boat *Three Sisters*. She had been built of oak at Thorpeness in 1896 and Percy Westrup and Tim Brown had worked her off the beach there until 1952. After this she had become a work-boat at Orford and the current owner, Ralph Brinkley, said it had been his father's boat and he did not wish to sell it.

I thought of Thorpeness again and I returned to find that Harry Harling and Percy Westrup had gone to better fishing grounds and their cottages had changed hands. However, abandoned on the beach, the 15ft sailing pot boat *Pet* looked as if she would be a likely candidate for the next November 5 bonfire. Again, she turned out to be 'father's boat' and the Wilson family all had to agree before we could buy her.

Eventually the hulk was collected from the beach and taken back to Frank Knights' yard at Woodbridge. We had a battle with the shipwrights because they wanted to build us a new hull, rather than restore the 1902 *Pet*. In recent decades the yard had been building new wooden boats with powerful diesel engines to fish off Aldeburgh beach and they could see no point in fitting throles (wooden pegs to hold the oars). We insisted she was to have all her fittings exactly as these punts had in the Edwardian photographs.

The photographs showed that the mizzens had several rows of reef points, but our sail maker said 'you only need one set of reef points in that little mizzen because it will obviously be your first reef.' The old photographs were right, a Suffolk punt would not sail properly without a mizzen set, there was a need for several rows of reef points.

While in Southwold with *L'Atalanta* in August 1981, fisherman Ernie Stannard appeared and said 'are you the people who have done up one of our boats? Well you are doing it all wrong'. His father had been the Southwold champion when racing the punt *Smiling Morn* and he told us that all her proper gear, including the leeboard, was hanging up as decoration in the 'Bell' Inn at Walberswick. The only man we knew of who had sailed a Southwold punt was John 'Dusso' Wilson, sometime mayor of that lovely town, and he maintained it was quicker to row to windward than to try and sail!

In the autumn Jim Lawrence came over with his drift net and we went out after herring in *Pet*. We began to understand the layout of the boat and bit by bit we re-learned some of the forgotten secrets of sailing the little dipping lugger. We still dreamed of the *Three Sisters* and after five years of negotiations Ralph agreed to give us the hulk if I bought her old engine. Following this, the hulk lay in a barn for six years while we were still sailing *L'Atalanta*. Our family were still teenage, but once they went off to lead their own lives Pearl and I began to find the big cutter too heavy to sail.

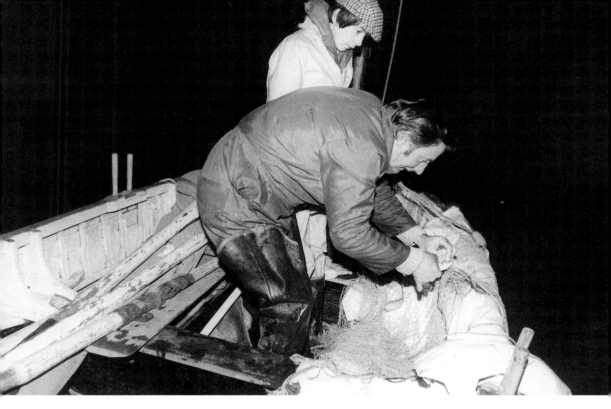

52. Herring drifting in the *Pet,* Jonathan and Jim Lawrence, 1981.

53. Jonathan rowing the *Pet* at Aldeburgh on a trip from Ramsholt to Snape, 1986.

Every spring I found it harder to find the energy to fit out a 35ft wooden boat. Either *L'Atalanta* was growing larger or I was getting older. Two incidents signed the decision to part with my beloved cutter. Every year I used to haul Pearl up the mast in a bos'n's chair and she would come down slowly varnishing the mast with her hands. One year when we had just finished she quietly and firmly said that she was not going up the mast again. The other time, we were bashing into a sea off Walton Naze when Bob More came up on deck and said the water was over the cabin floor.

54. Caroline and Jonathan sailing the *Pet* in Hollesley Bay, 1986.

Most years we used to take *L'Atalanta* up to one of the Woodbridge boatyards for expensive repair work. If I continued spending money on the cutter I could never have the longshore boat rebuilt, one of them had to go and it was not an easy choice. In the end I went for rebuilding *Three Sisters*, but there was a further delay. Frank Knights' yard took on the work, but they had restarted building open longshore boats. In 1991 they built the 19ft *Dodger* for 'Dodger' Holmes to fish professionally off Dunwich beach. She will probably be the last wooden boat built to work off the Suffolk beaches, because in 1995 the fishermen began trying cheaper fibreglass hulls. However, Knights built two more wooden boats while my old hulk lay in their boat park looking uncomfortably like a pile of firewood. Finally I spoke to Frank Knights, although officially retired, who said 'I will make sure they do your boat this winter'. Shortly after this there was a phone call from the yard to say work had started and would I come down and say what I wanted done.

The hulk had been laid up in Brinkley's yard for about twenty years and at the start she had been covered with a tilt, but this had partly blown off and the area reached by the rain-water had rotted. The keel was completely rotten, so 'Little John' White made moulds so that we did not lose the shape. There is a great deal of moral dilemma in the traditional boat world if you totally rebuild a hull, as to whether you still have the same craft. The old hull was pulled to pieces, was burned to recover the copper nails, and a new hull rose in its place so that she lived on.

Longshore fishermen who dropped in to Knights' yard watched the progress and one remarked 'Now you are building a proper boat'. Billy Burrell, Aldeburgh fisherman and lifeboat coxswain, really surprised me when he said '*Three Sisters* was the fastest boat we had (Aldeburgh and Thorpeness), when she raced in our beach regatta she was hauled up on the beach before any of the other boats had finished. Just look how fine she is aft, that's why she is fast.'

The more recent Suffolk motor longshore boats were built to be powered by a powerful diesel and had higher sides than *Three Sisters*, but they were much more lightly built, no doubt to make them cheaper. We insisted that our rebuild was as strong as the original hull. John White said in horror 'this boat is only 18ft long, but it's got thirty-one knees!' and Andy added quietly 'there is more work putting in the knees than building the rest of the boat'.

55. Jonathan finding the hulk of *Three Sisters* at Orford in 1980.

When sailing *Pet* hard off St Peter's flats at the mouth of the River Blackwater in the 1992 East Coast Old Gaffers' Race, she had pulled the foremast step out and the lug fore-sail had collapsed over the bow. It happened very quickly and was the most frightening situation that we had experinced in a lugger. Until the squall passed we could not get the sail down and it felt as if at any moment she would go over. Later we realised that had she gone over, all our lifejackets would have been trapped in the bow. This taught us that a big lug foresail on the mainmast put great pressure on the hull and it had to be stepped very strongly to the keel.

Some of the 1896 knees, thumb cleats and copper nails were good enough to go back into the new Norfolk larch hull. The old hull with sailing stern had leaked once the motor had been put in, so the new stern had to be built to take the 10 hp diesel engine. The Suffolk punts never had a centreboard, but we rated an engine more important.

On a cold spring day in 1990 we had sailed the *Pet* from Slaughden Quay on the River Alde some nineteen miles round to the Rocks Reach on the Deben. There was a fresh breeze, perhaps too fresh for the little 15 footer. Going out of the River Ore with the ebb we bounced through choppy water on the bar at Shingle Street, but averaged about 4.5 knots for the trip. However we only achieved this because Robert Brinkley kindly gave us a tow, only for about 100 yards, but this was through the fierce ebb coming around the point near the Felixstowe Ferry Sailing Club. We could have made the passage under sail, but we would have had to anchor, as the sailing barges used to, and wait for the tide to change in our favour.

At Easter, 1994 with a snowstorm blowing across the Ferry Quay, our granddaughter Laura relaunched *Three Sisters* by breaking an Easter egg on the bow. After the launching we took parties of friends out for little trips down the river and one quayside expert on the Ferry Dock grumbled that the boat had been dangerously over-loaded. Obviously he did not rate the Suffolk beach boat very highly, but Billy Burrell had told us that they reck-oned to load 'four tons of herring' in an 18ft boat and often they rowed them back to the beach with just the top plank above the water.

To prevent the catch moving around, the sailing boats had the inside hull divided by planks into 'fish rooms', but these were the only original fitting we left out. The two-masted dipping lug rig suited the fishermen because they could go off the beach on one tack and come back on the other. It was very important for an open boat at sea that the foresail halliard was always ready to be cast off in a sudden squall so the lugsail would come down at once. Also, when the drift nets were being worked, the foresail could be stowed out of the way, while in a gaff-rigged boat the boom was always in the way. They used to say you could always tell an old Essex smackman because he was bent double after years of bending under the boom.

Any boat is a compromise, Pearl and I wanted a traditional day boat that we could sail together, and the lug rig suited us because on family motoring trips we stowed the sail out of the way leaving plenty of room. Our little lugger proved to be such a successful day boat for coastal cruising that we were surprised no one else ordered another hull from Knights. John White cleared us up on this point with a breezy 'you're happy with the boat because you are an eccentric!'

Thirty years before I had been 'out of date' by sticking to the gaff rig, but it seems that by keeping to a wooden hull I reached the full state of eccentricity. John went on to explain 'you see they are training wooden boatbuilders at Lowestoft, but no one is training people to be wooden boat owners'. Our wooden hull proved much cheaper than the fibreglass

56. Laura Southernwood launching *Three Sisters* with an Easter Egg at the Ferry Quay, Woodbridge in 1994.

'classics' which are mass-produced, but many people coming into leisure sailing lack the confidence to go for a wooden hull.

Jonathan and I always hoped that more people would take up the cause and restore other Suffolk longshore boats, but if you start a forest fire it is difficult to predict which way it will go. In 1992 I was approached by the Reverend Mountney who had read about the restoration of *Pet* and liked the idea. I took the Mountneys for a sail in her up the Deben. I was very keen to show the dipping lug in a favourable light and fortunately we reached up the river through the Stonner Channel to Methersgate Quay where the tide and wind turned. We only dipped the lug once and then reached back again.

The Rev Mountney was not fooled, but took up the basic principle of the shallow beamy Suffolk punt and had Paul Fisher design him a modern version with a centreboard and gaff rig, which he sails from Craster. The drawings of this boat were seen by Kevin Halcrow of Lakeland Wooden Boats and he began building a 16ft Suffolk Beach Punt class.

57. New hull, new sails and learning new skills with handling a dipping lugger, the very new *Three Sisters* on the Deben in 1994.

After sailing decked craft all my life, I was apprehensive about the first long sea trip in an open boat. We went out of the Deben an hour before low water to take the flood tide south to Maldon about thirty miles away. It was blowing about force 4-5 off the land and at first we did not notice the wind, but as we drew away from the land under power and sail the full force of the wind was such that Jonathan and Martin had to have the foresail down to put in reefs. The beamy hull gave her buoyancy to   bounce over the seas rather than go through them, as a bigger boat would have done. I had heard stories of Aldeburgh boats being caught six miles off-shore in the middle of winter loaded with cod and having to battle back and land on the beach through breaking waves. Some were swamped when beaching, but the greatest danger is, when trawling, if they catch on a 'fast' and are pulled over.

The passage to Maldon was calm as long as we stayed close under the land past Walton and Clacton, but after rounding Colne Point we met a short angry little sea in the River Blackwater thrown up by the wind over tide. We motored straight into this and it was very lively and wet. The top of the Blackwater was the worst as the boat banged into short seas and to avoid this I cut inside Osea Island. Back in the main channel off Northey Island we met up with a couple of smacks throwing up spray as they motored up to the 'Maldon Traditional Sail 94' event. We arrived at Hythe Quay at high water, past the lofty barges and brightly-painted smacks with their varnished masts and long bowsprits and berthed in one of Noddy Cardy's docks.

In our first season with *Three Sisters* we visited the head of most of the rivers and large creeks between Blythburgh and Maldon. The longest sea trip Jonathan and I have done in *Three Sisters* was the thirty-five mile passage in 1996 to take part in the first Lowestoft Smack Race for about a century. The passage bore out the local weather lore that the weather patterns change with the tides, although expert weather people claim this cannot possibly happen. We motored round Orfordness in a flat lifeless sea and reached Thorpeness at high water. Then, just as the ebb started, a strong squall from the NE brought in heavy rain, we hurriedly pulled on oilskins as the boat slammed into the angry sea. The tide swept us past Southwold and I looked longingly at the sheltered waters of the tiny harbour inside the pier.

The sea was building up and I thought it could just be unwise to continue on to Lowestoft, but we were determined to make the first smack race since 1892. As a reward for our perseverance the weather cleared when we reached the crumbling sandy cliffs of Covehithe. We had just hauled off our clammy oilskins when the sailing barge *Cabby* swept past bound south and skipper Gerard Swift shouted out that he was using sail and motor to arrive on time for an important charter. We eventually reached the Trawl Basin at Lowestoft where *Three Sisters* was dwarfed by high quays and huge steel trawlers. Apparently these were Dutch-owned, but since they were fishing on a British quota they had to spend a certain number of days in a British port.

The weather was very blustery during the following week and the actual race was more of a celebration of Lowestoft's fishing heritage than a competitive sailing race. In *Three Sisters* we bobbed about in lumpy seas without making the slightest progress against the North Sea. The Essex smacks did not do much better, only the *Sallie* actually got round the course. It was a day for the big trawling ketches. Lowestoft's own *Excelsior* and the Swedish *Atlantica* and *Gratitude* really liked the breeze and sailed powerfully around the course.

Just as everyone was heading back for the Trawl Basin, the 79ft *Deodar* arrived from

Stockholm. We had sailed in *Deodar* at Stockholm a few years earlier and there were no worries about tide there. Her owner, Thomas Hellstrom, just cast off when he was ready and we sailed toward the islands of the archipelago. This smack had been sold away from Lowestoft fifty years before and descendants of those who had owned and sailed on her gave her a warm welcome on her return. Thomas, a gentle man, even though his great mass of hair made him look like a marauding Viking, was not happy with North Sea tides. He wondered why he had left the peaceful tideless water of the Stockholm archipelago.

My worst experience with *Three Sisters* has not been in the North Sea, but in rural Somerset! In 1997 Pearl and I were taking her on a trailer to the Looe Lugger Regatta when the wheel bearing and axle burnt out. This was at a narrow part of the A30 and heavy traffic thundered by while I struggled unsuccessfully to get the wheel studs off. I felt that at any moment my boat would be reduced to firewood. We arrived at the Looe Lugger Regatta with our boat on a lorry, not the cheapest way of travelling. It then blew a gale for three days and we did not even get outside the harbour.

The Looe Lugger Regatta was started in 1989 to encourage people to restore the decked Cornish luggers. When we first went in 1995, Devon luggers from Beer did the serious small boat racing. It was a good chance to meet up with lugger expert Alan Abbot, whose father and grandfather had fished with luggers from the little pebbly beach at Beer. On our first visit to Looe two years before, the star had been Jon and Judy Brickhill's 40ft Looe-built lugger *Guide Me*. The Brickhills have sailed their dipping lugger all over the North Atlantic without an engine. At Looe they did not accept a friendly tow from one of the other luggers with engines, but tacked up to the tiny entrance under the towering cliff, and warped themselves up the harbour to the quay.

When racing in Looe Bay, the *Guide Me* made dipping the forelug look easy, but it calls for good timing and a good crew. On the Cornish lugger the foresail is dipped by passing the head of the yard around the forward side of the mast, but on most decked luggers the sail is lowered and man-handled around the mast and then rehoisted. Lowering and shifting around the mast was the method used aboard Hobson Rankin's Scottish 43ft fifie *Isabella Fortuna* when we sailed on the River Tay. This black fifie had been built in 1890 for summer line fishing off the east coast of Scotland. On her we beat up the Tay past the bonnie City of Dundee. Frankly, carrying the yard and sail around the mast on each tack was very heavy work, and Hobson had restored *Isabella* as a cruising yacht and made voyages around the north of Scotland. Last time I heard from him he had a bad back. You have really got to love a lugger to sail one.

The one good point about a dipping lugger is the simplicity of its gear, the very point that fishermen in the days of sail found so useful. You can run a small lugger ashore and pack the gear in a matter of seconds. We found this really useful when we took *Pet* on a trailer to the great traditional boat rally of 'Brest 92'. Here in the wide harbour, home of the French Navy, was every traditional work boat type you had ever dreamt of and a lot more besides. We stood open-mouthed in wonder as a nippy three-masted bisquine, the cream of the lugger family, was skilfully tacked in and out of Brest Harbour. We were not just impressed with the beauty of these craft, but with the fact that they existed at all. Fourteen years before we had travelled around Brittany searching for its famous working craft. We had found very little, the only bisquine had been the hulk of the *Egalite* rotting away in the sand dunes near Lancieux. Since then, Brittany has recreated its maritime past and built ninety-seven replicas of former working craft. I did feel that after decades of searching I had reached some kind of old work boat Valhalla.

We returned to France with the *Three Sisters,* to take part in 'Douarneney 1996'. The previous winter I had filled in forms and sent off faxes, in English and then French, trying to find out details about this event. We received no information, although at one point a plank arrived from Brest with an invitation to paint a picture on it.

We arrived at this huge international festival of the sea to find most of the old fishing town of Douarneney had been closed to all traffic. This discovery was made at the bottom of a one-way street at the foot of a hill. In the baking heat Jonathan showed great driving skill when he backed *Three Sisters* on her trailer up the hill. The local drivers were little impressed with his skills as we had brought this end of the town to a standstill. We returned to our bed and breakfast, where the gallant Madame Odette Boulic, a lady not in the first flush of youth, ordered us to follow her car to the neighbouring town of Trebol. We arrived at a barricade which at first would not let us through, Madame Boulic launched into forceful French and after a fine display of Gallic bravado on both sides the barricade was removed. We arrived at a small harbour where there were very good facilities, all laid on free and very friendly, for unloading. Douarneney is such a vast event that I suppose there were not the resources to send out information to individual boats.

The harbour and its bay were beautiful and we were told there were over a thousand traditional boats from all over Europe and about two million visitors. At times, the quays in the old town were very crowded and it felt as if half the French population was there. We decided one day to sail about five miles across the bay and find a peaceful place. It

58. The bisquine *Cancalaise* in Douarneney Bay, 1997.

was a wonderful family outing. Caroline and Clive and their children Laura and Thomas, Jonathan and Clare and baby Harry, on his first trip at sea, slept in the bottom of the boat. We sailed until we found an almost empty bay. Just a single lady with two small children and only one caravan on the cliff top, this was the place for us.

As we sorted out the anchor Clive came back and said 'That lady knows your name, the boat's name and thinks you have sailed across the bay to meet her!'

Pearl gave me a very suspicious glance as I set out to meet this attractive young French woman. It turned out that the organisers had allocated a French family to be the host for each of the visiting boats. Our information had been given to the Urvois family of Brest and we had landed quite by chance at the summer holiday beach they owned at Kervigan. Our bows had touched the beach just in front of Dominique Urvois as if the whole event had been carefully planned.

That evening Pearl and I joined Max and Dominique Urvois and their friends for a barbecue on the clifftop and I offered to take them all for a sail. The next day Pearl and I sailed *Three Sisters* across to Kervigan and although it was not rough we arrived to find a heavy ground swell rolling up the beach. We anchored off and tried to signal by waving that there was too much breaking water.

Dominique swam through the breaking waves and hung on to the side of boat while we explained in a funny mixture of French and English why we could not land. Dominique said 'I will tell Max' and was off back through the rollers to the beach. We saw the families standing having a conference, then they all entered the water and swam out to us with their small children on their backs hanging on to their necks. Getting them all aboard was a major panic, the lady from the second family bruised her legs, but once they were all in we hoisted sail and headed out into the bay.

The two French families were all perfectly happy swimming in the breaking waves, but the movement of the boat starting to leave the land worried them. When we returned to the beach they all quickly leapt overboard like seals returning to their natural element.

59. The only change we have made to *Three Sisters* traditional dipping lug rig is a brail on the mizzen and a stay on each side, 1998.

Chapter Ten

WHITE HORSES ON THE BAR

Jonathan became very restless during the seven hour passage in *Three Sisters* back from the first revival Lowestoft Smack Race. On a larger craft there is always a slight change of scenery by going below to rest or to make a cup of tea, but on an open boat you just have to sit there in all weathers. There was more to it than that. The previous winter he had bought the 22ft Great Yarmouth shrimper *Crangon* and the sight of the smacks racing had made him wish that she was ready to be sailed too.

For a time he had been keen on car-rallying, but returned to sailing when he took Clare on their honeymoon in *Three Sisters* up the coast to Southwold and finally fulfilled his dream of buying a winkle brig. The true winkle brig was an open clinker gaff sloop once used by West Mersea fishermen for the creeks and mouth of the River Blackwater. We had bought the 15ft *Mary Agnes,* a boat I had seen being built by Alf Last at Cooks at Maldon in 1971.

Alf Last had been fourteen when he started work at the yard on a month's trial, but Mr Walter Cook was very firm that he would not have a regular job until he could prove he was up to the job. Fifty-one years later he was still building boats in the same shed and he said 'no one has told me yet whether I've got the job permanently'.

Gordon Swift, then part-owner of Cooks, had suggested to Alf that he should go on the beach, measure up Gerard Swift's successful racing winkle brig *Winnie* and build two replicas. Alf must have forgotten the measurements when walking back to the shed because the *Mary Agnes* was nothing like *Winnie.* Anyway, Alf was a renowned clinker boat builder, but his '14ft barge's boats' were never two the same length.

The *Mary Agnes* was not really large enough for Jonathan and Clare's young family so a larger wooden fishing boat was sought and found. This was the *Crangon,* a Great Yarmouth shrimper built in 1957 with an engine, but she also had a full suit of sails. This was the same year that I had bought *Sea Fever* and I had no idea that sail-using fishing boats were then still being built in East Anglia. She had been lying just up river of Yarmouth Customs House when I had set off with *L'Atalanta* in 1970, never dreaming that a generation later I would be bringing her down the coast as well.

Gus Lee and Boswell on the North River at Yarmouth had in the 1950s built a 20ft shrimper called *Shiner,* but the engine took up too much of the working space. So, when Fred Symonds wanted a new boat to replace his 1907 19ft *Horace & Hannah,* he asked their shipwright Billy Steward to built him the 22ft hull, 9ft beam half-decked clinker *Crangon.* The name came from the Latin word for her chief quarry, the brown shrimp, and some of the timber was seven hundred year old oak out of a Great Yarmouth church which had been bombed during World War II.

No power tools were used, every plank was hand-sawn by Steward and his apprentice. Another fisherman who saw *Crangon* said he would have a bigger version, but Steward said 'this one's big enough for you' and built him a sister ship, the *Boy Frank,* from the same moulds. Both Symond's and Moore's new shrimpers used their sails for a few years. The skipper of *Betsey,* who was also shrimping at this time, told us they all had sails and used them 'to blow home when they had been trawling off Cromer', but when the sails wore out they were not replaced and the masts and bowsprits were cut down.

60. Fred Symonds trawling in *Crangon* for shrimps off Great Yarmouth beach in 1989.

When Fred Symonds retired, he kept his boat for part-time fishing. In 1989, with the Husseys, we wanted to make a documentary film about the old style fishing and Fred, then in his eighties, took us out shrimping. I did not hear of the *Crangon* again until 1996 when Jonathan asked me to go to see her lying for sale in Newson's yard at the top of Lake Lothing. Her appearance had changed completely and it was very good luck that she was not sawn up in the 'decommission' scam. Yarmouth fisherman John Wells had fitted a wheelhouse, but she was really too small and elderly for commercial fishing. John Wells would have sold her fish quota as well, but that was worth more than the boat.

Jonathan bought *Crangon* and commissioned to haul her out onto the slip and be checked. From Lowestoft we had a lonely trip on a brisk March day, motoring against the wind to the Deben. While the Thames Estuary is full of craft, above Orfordness we only saw *Dodger* crosssing in front of us as she returned to Dunwich beach from fishing. Huddled in the wheelhouse we muttered that this terrible structure would be the first to go when she was converted to a sailing craft. The Woodbridge shipwright JK beefed-up the *Crangon's* hull. After forty years in the rain the foredeck and thwarts had to be replaced and the hull strengthened to take the pressure from the mast.

I have always kept a store of old wooden blocks, spars and sails hidden in my garden shed. Suddenly I discovered they had almost vanished and that I had donated them to the restoration of the *Crangon*. One thing I would not part with was *Sea Fever's* oil riding light. I had bought this from Whitmore's, the barge chandlers on Ipswich Dock, in 1957 and had used it throughout my boating career.

It took two years to get *Crangon* sailing properly. This included mastering the Yarmouth shrimper's characteristic upright-jackyard topsail. Setting a topsail is often a source of trouble aboard a gaff boat, in fact the only thing I have found which is more nuisance on a boat, is a fox terrier.

In 1998 we set back up the coast in *Crangon* to the first Southwold Sole Bay Race and another Lowestoft Smack Race. It was an unsettled June day as we motored down the Deben and the wind appeared to be rising. As we motored out of the haven, the sea looked grey and unwelcoming. Twice in the channel over the bar she buried her long bowsprit into a steep wall of water. The open sea was lumpy, the result of a force 5 southerly against a flood tide coming down from the north. Jonathan lost his peaked cap while setting a tiny jib and the mainsail with all four reefs down. 'What do you think', said the hatless owner 'we go on to Southwold?'

This was the roughest sea we had tried *Crangon* in, if it proved too much we could pop over the bar at Shingle Street and get into the safe haven of the River Ore. All the same, I steered north away from the land towards Orfordness lighthouse, the local Cape Horn. Orfordness is a twelve mile long shingle wilderness with a white and red lighthouse on the point of the Ness. Just before the Ness there are some overfalls on the ebb, I have never been there in bad weather, but from a distance it is just a white mass of very dangerous breaking waves.

The *Crangon*, apart from the cuddy forward, is open so as we came to round the Ness lighthouse not a word was spoken. The tide was still flooding and it was blowing force 6 by then, making an impressive sea, but we did not once take any water over the sides. By the time we passed Aldeburgh the tide was ebbing and the seas slightly smaller. The tension eased and we started to talk again. Jonathan thought we might make a good photograph when entering Southwold Harbour and called Pearl on his mobile to nip up ahead and be ready on the piers.

61. Jonathan at the tiller of the *Crangon* in a lumpy sea off Orfordness, 1998.

We gybed off Southwold and as we approached the narrow entrance to the harbour, John Buckley and Marcus came out to see us in, with an inflatable. They looked worried, but then they knew what was waiting for us in the harbour mouth of this bar haven. Once between the piers we were thrown sideways by a series of fierce waves, the result of the ebb rushing out of the harbour and hitting the tide, which was forging along the coast. It took the two of us on the tiller to keep her on course. Between the piers there is no room to turn and we rode on a crest of white water into the peaceful harbour. Above us, amongst the crowd on the pier, we caught a glimpse of Pearl with the camera.

Hanging up in the bar of the Southwold Sailing Club is a copy of a poster for the 1850 Southwold Regatta with prize money of £3 for the first 'Beach Punt', enough then to build a new boat. My own beach punt, the *Three Sisters,* remained back on the Deben, while I had become crew on the *Crangon*. Races for punts and traditional craft at Southwold had faded out in the 1920s, so after a gap of nearly seventy years, nineteen smacks and other similar craft went out of the harbour for the first Sole Bay Race.

The day was grey and drizzly, but the force 4 southerly was a superb breeze for racing around buoys off the town. The roar of the surf on the beach could be heard, while steam rose up from Adnams brewery in the centre of the town, behind the lighthouse. Both sights to cheer a sailor's heart. The bawley *Bona,* well handled under a cloud of sail, won, while in *Crangon* our owner was pleased to be placed fourteenth. The other Yarmouth shrimper, the 19ft *Horace & Hannah*, was short of a crew and had not raced.

62. The *Crangon* entering Southwold in a breeze, 1998.

63. Lowering the *Crangon's* topsail as she ghosts into Lowestoft Harbour, 1998.

Only a few craft continued north up the coast to Lowestoft for the smack race there. It was a relaxed hazy day, but we could easily pick out the white pagodas on either side of the narrow harbour mouth. As we approached under sail one man on the pier got quite excited and shouted 'keep you acoming!' but he had used all his film long before we reached the pier heads. We sailed on, Jonathan dropped the topsail and then cast off the peak halliard so that the sail and gaff folded down against the mast while I held the helm guiding us right into the Trawl Basin. Shortly afterwards Graham Hussey came in with the *Horace & Hannah* and quietly remarked that he would be racing with a crew the next day. The clock had been put back and for the first time for about a century shrimpers were racing off the East Anglian coast.

The actual race was something of an anti-climax. There was very little wind and the local yacht club had set us a course against a light wind and strong tide. The local fibreglass yachts slowly fought their way south against the tide towards Pakefield while we in the small traditional boat class were swept north by the tide through Lowestoft Roads. The yacht club officials were not impressed, and arrived in a powerful launch with instructions that we must sail the proper course. A shouting match developed and we demanded a new course, which seemed a good idea as our class was just about to be swept on to the breaking water of the Holme Sands.

A new course was devised and the launch roared off, leaving us drifting north. The other traditional boats gave up, but there was no way that we or the *Horace & Hannah* were going to. We tacked inshore under Lowestoft Ness, the most easterly point of the British Isles, and let go the anchor to prevent us from drifting further north. Graham in the *Horace & Hannah* just made headway against the tide and kept battling on, tacking almost into the breakwaters and gaining a few feet each time. It took over three hours for him to beat back to the finishing line. Once the tide turned, we hauled up the anchor and in thirty-five minutes tacked back to the finish off the south harbour pier.

The next day was something of a pilgrimage, because Jonathan wanted to take the *Crangon* about ten miles up the coast to the Great Yarmouth quay where she had been based for nearly forty years. In Yarmouth, we counted four modern fishing boats with shrimp trawls aboard, but before 1914 there had been sixty-five of these little sailing shrimpers working from Yarmouth and Gorleston. We understood why they had stuck with their half-deckers. The shrimpers could be either tacked or rowed up this narrow harbour, while a large decked craft would not have been nearly as easy to handle in the river.

We were impressed that after rounding the Bush Bend into Yarmouth's two mile long commercial harbour, one of the Williments appeared on the quay with a camera, the sole witness to the brief homecoming of one of the last of the town's shrimpers. The Williments run a ships' chandlers and net supplying business from a nineteenth century brick ware-house in Gorleston. We had bought a beam trawl from them back in the winter and had listened to stories from the founder of the business, Paul Williment, as he sat by the fire, making nets and telling us about Norfolk boats past and present.

We motored up to Haven Bridge where *Crangon* used to berth. I climbed up on to the quay and departed to buy fish and chips and returned to find *Crangon* almost unbearable in the tropical heat. For flood protection Yarmouth Harbour was lined with steel piles and in the narrow river on a hot June day this became a windless canyon. When we left it was good to get out into the fresh breezes of the open sea, Yarmouth's infamous bad entrance was very peaceful, just brown water from the Norfolk Broads flowing out to meet the clear blue water of the North Sea.

After sailing down the coast we called Lowestoft Harbour Radio for permission to re-enter and mentioned 'returning from Yarmouth', the port's ancient rival. The voice on the radio changed tone and added quickly 'you'll need customs clearance coming from *the other place.*'

Some things may stay the same, but mostly the coast and its people are changing all the time. Back in Lowestoft we berthed at the new Heritage Quay, reserved just for tradi-tional boats. This is something new, the old work boats have become part of the region's cultural identity. When we departed from Lowestoft Harbour to return to the Deben it was raining hard and for a while the Suffolk coast was just a faint black line on our starboard side. In Sole Bay the sun came out and we passed the Dunwich longshore boat *Fred's Last,* trawling. Her owner gave us a cheerful wave as we passed by.

We were both well offshore, yet if we had been there a few centuries earlier we would have been at the entrance to Dunwich Harbour, which led to the town, now under the sea. To have sailed into that great harbour would have been wonderful. In fact for much of that passage down the coast we were passing over a seabed where medieval shepherds had once

64. Recreating the atmosphere of the great age of fishing under sail. The *Horace & Hannah*, *Crangon* and Leigh *Enterprise* in the Trawl Basin, Lowestoft, 1998.

65. Boys with their toys, RS, Caroline and Jonathan with *Three Sisters* and *Crangon* at the North Weir Point, River Ore on a Bawdsey Haven Yacht Club cruise. 1998. (*Clive Southernwood*)

grazed their flocks. The force of the sea has no respect for the plans of men ashore or afloat.

Round Orfordness we were straight into a stiff south-westerly and a short sea caused clouds of spray to rise over the bluff bow. The Deben bar was marked by a line of breaking water, except for the channel where there were short waves. Once in the haven we were surprised by the amount of water to be pumped out. We had a leak, so instead of picking up her mooring we ran *Crangon* up on the beach. Here at low tide the stern gland could be tightened up to solve the problem. It was a cold June day and the stiff wind was rustling the trees ashore. Another trip had ended, we had reached our intended destination.

FAMILY BOATS

Lassie 1H12. Open clinker boat about 18ft long built by Robertson, Woodbridge in 1924. First Shingle Street fishing boat to be built with an engine. Original owner Charles Lucock, named after his dog. Fell to pieces in King's Lynn dock about 1955.

Merry Princess. 28ft Norfolk Broads motor cruiser said to have been one of five named after royalty. Bought by Norman Simper at Wroxham in 1951, sold 1964 In the early 1980s was at Tollesbury under a different name.

Swallow. 12ft open clinker boat with standing lugsail built about 1935 for Mrs Wicken's children to sail on Thorpeness Meare. Bought by Norman Simper in 1951 as a tender for his motor cruiser *Merry Princess* and used by Robert Simper to learn to sail and explore on the River Deben. Sold to Frank Knights to be a ferry boat and fell to pieces at Woodbridge.

Lucky. 14ft Waldringfield SC Dragonfly class. Early numbers of the Dragonfly class were built by Ernie Nunn at Waldringfield. *Lucky* was the thirteenth Dragonfly built and the first by 'Robbie' Robertson at Lime Kiln Yard, Woodbridge but nobody would have the unlucky number 13 so she was number 14. She was kept at Ramsholt and raced at Waldringfield while owned by Robert Simper between 1954-57.

Sea Fever. 28ft long 9ft beam clinker double-ended ship's lifeboat bought by Ron Bayly of Felixstowe Ferry from a group lying in the Surrey Commercial Dock, had 37 carved on the bow, so she might have been built in 1937. Converted by Ron Bayly to a gaff cutter. Owned by Robert Simper 1957-70.

L'Atalanta. 35ft long 11ft beam and 5ft draught. Custom's cutter built at Landskrona, Sweden in 1904. Owned by Robert and Pearl Simper 1970-93. Sold to Frank Knights, who had set out to the Dunkirk Evacuation in 1940 aboard her, although the Admiralty stopped them at Ramsgate. Frank Knights (Shipwrights) Ltd tore out all the cabin accommodation and in 1998 she had a new deck fitted at Woodbridge.

Pet IH45. 15ft traditional Suffolk punt with dipping lug. Origin uncertain but was probably one of the work boats built in a shed at the back of Sudbourne 'Chequers' by wheelwright Mr Bugg. Registered as being built in 1902, but must have been rebuilt at least twice. Owned by several fishermen on the Suffolk coast. Once when she changed ownership was rowed in two days by 'Keydie' Wilson and another man from Lowestoft to Aldeburgh because they did not buy the sails. Bought by Jonathan Simper in 1981.

Three Sisters IH81. 18ft clinker Suffolk beach boat built, oak on oak with 'joggled' frames on to the planks, at Thorpeness in 1896 for Mr Ralph. Used for trawling in the summer and drifting in the winter. Total rebuild by Frank Knights (Shipwrights), Woodbridge in 1994.

Crangon YH55. Great Yarmouth shrimper 22ft long, 9ft beam and 3.6ft draft. Clinker half decker built in 1957. Built as a motor sailer. About 1991 bought by John Wells and fitted with a wheelhouse and stern gallows. Bought by Jonathan Simper in 1995 and converted to a sailing boat with traditional single headsail on a long bowsprit and a loose-footed mainsail on a pole boom.

Cockle. Mirror dinghy 4822 used by Caroline to learn to sail.

Wonder. A 10ft yacht's tender built by Leslie W. Harris at Burnham-on Crouch, possibly about 1930. Sails and rows very well and used by Jonathan to learn to sail. Has a dagger plate and lug sail.

Nautilus. A 17ft long 6.3ft beam Norwegian faering from Hardanget fjord built about 1947. A light rowing and spritsail boat given a home in the barn.

Thames Tub, a single person skulling boat from the Thames, of unknown origin. Hull found lying beside a barn in East Mersea.

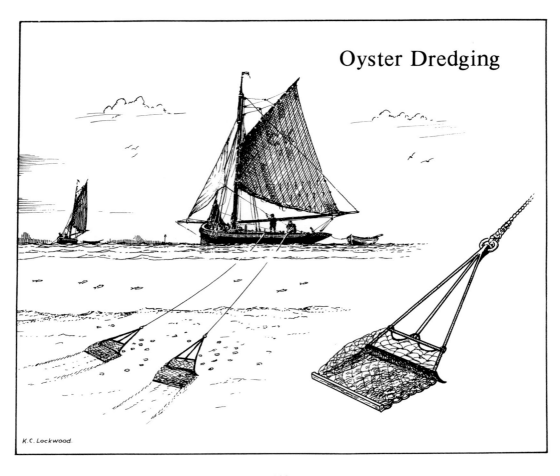

Oyster Dredging

K.C. Lockwood.